THE STORY OF
ANCIENT EGYPT

Fourth Edition

by

Suzanne Strauss Art

Wayside® PUBLISHING

waysidepublishing.com

This book is dedicated to the memory of my parents, Bernice Houston and Clifton Jean Strauss

Printed in USA

4 5 6 7 8 9 10 KP 22

Print date: 1369

ISBN 978-1-938026-54-6

CONTENTS

ACKNOWLEDGEMENTS

I wish to thank the following colleagues at Fay School for reading my manuscript: Dick Upjohn, Chairman of the Upper School History Department, Jillian Hensley, Director of Publications, and Mary Martin, Head of the Lower School. Their comments and encouragement were extremely helpful.

Special thanks go to my students at Fay—they were the source of my inspiration to write a lively book about ancient history in the first place. Their boundless enthusiasm for my project and their candid reactions to the chapters as I wrote them were key factors in the ultimate creation of a book that is proudly and unabashedly "kid-oriented."

Most of all, grateful appreciation and much love to my ever supportive family—my husband Bob and my children David and Robyn. They believed in the enterprise from the beginning and kept cheering me on through thick and thin until the book was finally ready for publication.

TO THE TEACHER

This book is based on many years of teaching ancient history to middle school students as well as a life-long fascination with the subject. For some time it has been clear to me that there is a great need for better classroom materials on ancient cultures at the middle school level (grades 5-8). Most textbooks tend to be superficial, bland and overly ambitious in the expanse of history they seek to cover. A middle school student can easily complete an amorphous volume entitled *The Ancient World* in a year's history course, but recent surveys (as well as my own observations) indicate that middle school students will remember very little of what he has read. Most trade books, on the other hand, are too narrowly focused to form the basis of a classroom unit. What is needed is a book that is both comprehensive in its treatment of a particular culture and sufficiently detailed to make the material meaningful to young readers. My book seeks to answer this need.

My teaching strategy is to present an overview of the geographical features and major historical periods of a culture and then to zero in on specific aspects of that culture, such as religion, art, science, and daily life. However, you might prefer to break up the long historical period covered in Chapter 3. For example, your students could read about the Old Kingdom and then move on to read the chapters on writing, religion, and the pyramids (the first section of Tombs and Temples). Later, they could return to Chapter 3 to read about the Middle Kingdom, following that with the chapter on mummies and burials. Finally, a reading of the New Kingdom could be followed by the chapters on science and math, daily life, and the second half of Tombs and Temples. Choose whichever scenario works best for you and your students.

The Story Of Ancient Egypt embodies my scholarly research on that phenomenally rich ancient civilization, augmented by my experience teaching the subject. I have endeavored to write in a style that is lively and crisp, using vocabulary that is provocative and occasionally challenging for the average middle school reader to grasp. The questions at the end of the chapters should help the students to review and clarify in their minds the material they have just read. Plentiful opportunities for discussions and enrichment activities are provided by the *Ideas To Think About* and *Further Thoughts* that follow the chapter questions. There is also a wealth of information about ancient Egyptian civilization readily available on the Internet. It should be a major resource for research projects.

Suzanne Strauss Art

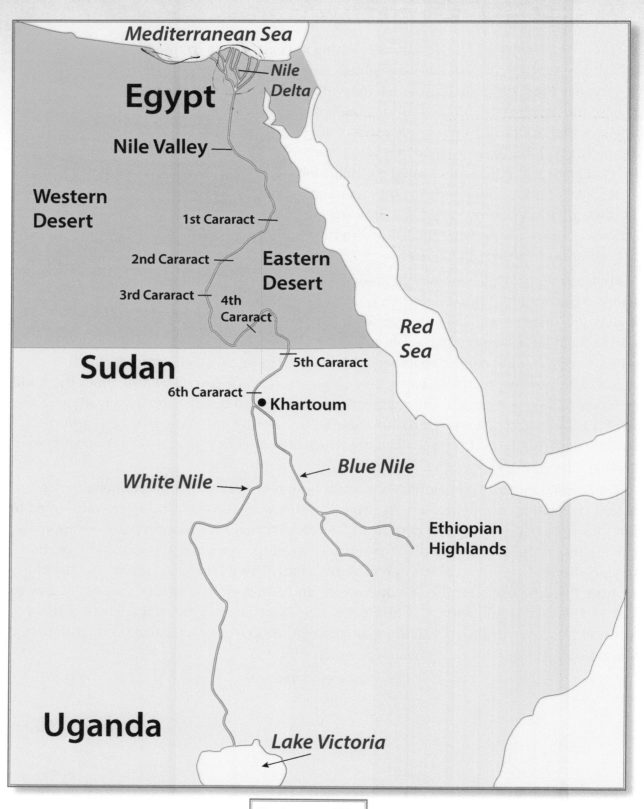

Mediterranean Sea

Nile Delta

Egypt

Nile Valley

Western Desert

1st Cararact

2nd Cararact

3rd Cararact

4th Cararact

Eastern Desert

Red Sea

5th Cararact

Sudan

6th Cararact

● Khartoum

White Nile

Blue Nile

Ethiopian Highlands

Uganda

Lake Victoria

Northeastern Africa

PROLOGUE

Imagine a land where the sky is always blue and cloudless, where the light of day becomes the darkness of night in a matter of minutes, where nearly all roads lead north or south, and where the people live much as their ancestors did thousands of years ago. Such a place is Egypt, a desert country in the northeast corner of Africa.

It is very hot in Egypt in the daytime, although the evening often ushers in refreshing breezes. The air is very dry. Less than one inch of rain falls on most parts of the country during an entire year. Snakes and lizards thrive among the desert's rocks and pebbles, but few people would want to live in such a barren and inhospitable environment were it not for the Nile River that flows gently through the center of the land.

The River Brings Life to the Desert

The Nile is the longest river in the world, covering a distance of over four thousand miles. It has two branches: the Blue Nile that originates in the mountains of Ethiopia, and the White Nile whose source is Lake Victoria in southern Uganda. The two branches join at the modern city of Khartoum in the Sudan. From there the river flows northward into Egypt, its narrow valley cutting through limestone hills for hundreds of miles until the terrain flattens. The valley is never more than twelve miles wide, and sometimes it measures only one mile. Just north of the city of Cairo the Nile splits into a maze of smaller rivulets that meander through green marshes until they finally empty into the

The banks of the Nile

Mediterranean Sea. This region is known as the delta.

The river is the habitat of many species of fish and waterfowl, not to mention crocodiles, and it serves as a major highway for boats. Thousands of years ago Egyptian farmers learned to channel the water of the Nile in order to grow their crops in the fertile soil along its banks, and their modern descendants continue to use many of the ancient methods to harvest grain and cotton there to this very day. The river is indeed a remarkable center of life and abundance in the middle of a desert wasteland. As early as the fifth century B.C.E. a famous Greek historian named Herodotus described Egyptian civilization as "the gift of the Nile."

possible quote

Natural Features Surround and Protect the Nile Valley

The desert covers over ninety-six percent of Egypt—in other words, everything that lies beyond the beneficent waters of the Nile. To the west are flat, rocky plains that extend to Libya, while to the east are low hills, many of them divided by dry riverbeds called *wadis*. Occasionally these fill with water after a heavy rain. Long ago, the *wadis* were major stopping points on the trade routes across the eastern deserts from the Nile valley to the coast of the Red Sea.

Egypt's unique geography made it possible for a rich civilization to flourish there for nearly three thousand years until just before the birth of Christ. The blistering heat of the desert to the east and west, the vastness of the sea as well as the swampy marshland to the north, and the perilous rapids and waterfalls (called cataracts) along the southern stretches of the Nile all served as natural buffers that effectively isolated the Egyptian people and protected them from invasion by foreign armies. In fact, during a period of two thousand years Egypt was invaded only three times! Because the Egyptians felt safe and secure in the Nile Valley, they did not concern themselves with national defense as other ancient peoples were forced to do. Rather, they were free to channel their energies in constructive ways. A hard-working and optimistic race, they created the world's first great centralized civilization – one that lasted longer, relatively unchanged, than any other.

A Nile dweller.

Why Study Ancient Egypt?

Although the civilization of ancient Egypt came to an end over two thousand years ago, it is of great interest to modern scholars. Many ideas and objects that we take for granted today can be traced back to the early dwellers of the Nile. For example, basic concepts of geometry, mathematics, and astronomy were first understood and used by Egyptian engineers. The columns that adorn our state buildings can be traced back to early Egyptian architecture. Great fortresses with battlements and drawbridges were built on Egypt's southern boundary nearly three thousand years before similar castles housed the lords and ladies of the Middle Ages. Egyptian workers constructed some of the largest stone structures in the world, many of which exist to this day. The Great Pyramid at Giza is enormous. It was built carefully and systematically by thousands of laborers. Just think of the organizational skills needed to accomplish such a task.

Those resourceful people of the Nile were the first to:

- domesticate cats and honey bees
- train carrier pigeons
- tan leather
- make glass
- design mosquito netting
- construct large canals and reservoirs
- survey land
- write on paper
- study human anatomy
- create a solar calendar
- use a scientific method of investigation based on direct observation

people of the nile were first to...

They also created myths about the origins of life and, for a short time, practiced a religion based upon worship of a single god, something very much ahead of their time.

Keys to Learning about Ancient Egypt

We know a great deal about the ancient Egyptians because the dry desert air has preserved the messages they wrote upon their scrolls of papyrus (a kind of paper), painted on the walls of their tombs and engraved upon their monuments. Similarly, the dry heat has preserved and protected their artifacts (tools, weapons, and objects of art) and even their human remains, so that they still appear much as they did when they were buried in the sand thousands of years ago. Modern technology has given archaeologists very efficient methods and devices for detecting long forgotten tombs and statues, and new discoveries are continually being made.

By studying these clues from the past, we can begin to imagine what it was like to live in the Nile Valley thousands of years ago. As we learn more about the ancient Egyptians, we will find many aspects of their culture that were very different from our own. For starters, compared to the fast pace of our twenty-first century high-tech global society, life along the Nile might seem to move in slow motion. Yet, the basic sensibilities and aspirations of the ordinary people will seem familiar. After all these centuries, human nature has changed very little, and by studying the past we can also learn a great deal about ourselves and the workings of the modern world. So, let's begin!

Questions

1. What are the sources of the Nile?
2. Why did Herodotus call Egypt "the gift of the Nile"?
3. Describe Egypt's natural buffers.
4. List five contributions the Egyptians made to our civilization.
5. How do we know about the ancient Egyptians?

Further Thoughts

1. There are many ways to visualize the extremely long time period during which the civilization of ancient Egypt flourished. One way is to draw a line on the white board that is two feet long. If one foot represents one thousand years, the entire line encompasses everything that has happened since the birth of Christ. Think of all the discoveries and changes that have taken place in the world during all those years! Now draw a line that is three feet long alongside the first line. This represents the civilization of ancient Egypt. As we shall learn, during these three thousand years most aspects of art, language, religion, government, the economy, and daily life in Egypt changed hardly at all! Ancient Egypt is thus remarkable not only for the vastness of its time frame but also for the stability of its culture.

Another way to think about time is to let one day represent a century. Using this formula, the history of America, beginning with the discoveries of the European explorers, would take five days. Using the same formula, the history of ancient Egypt would occupy an entire month!

2. A river delta derives its name from the fourth Greek letter (delta), which is written as a triangle. The maze of rivulets that empty the water of the Nile into the Mediterranean resemble the Greek letter when viewed from above (look at fig. 1). There are many other famous deltas in the world: for example, the delta of the Mississippi River near New Orleans and the delta of the Indus River in Pakistan.

3. Historians traditionally used the letters B.C. and A.D. to date events. Using the birth of Christ as a convenient breaking point, everything before that event, and counting backwards, was B.C. For example, twenty years before Christ was born was 20 B.C. A.D. referred to the year Christ was born. A.D. stands for Anno Domini, Latin for The Year of Our Lord. So everything after the birth of Christ was written with the letters A.D. In recent years, historians have begun replacing B.C. and A.D. with the letters B.C.E. (Before the Common Era) and C.E. (Common Era). These are the letters used in this book.

Projects

1. Herodotus was a famous Greek historian who visited ancient Egypt. As we have learned, he called Egypt "the gift of the Nile." He is known as the Father of History. Find out more about him, consulting books in your library as well as the Internet, and write a short report.

2. Study the map at the beginning of this section. Then draw your own map of northeastern Africa. Make a mileage scale, compass rose, and a key to indicate mountains, deserts and cataracts. Label the following: Cairo, Khartoum, the Nile, the White Nile, the Blue Nile, Lake Victoria, the Red Sea, the Mediterranean Sea, the Delta, the six cataracts, Egypt, the Sudan, Uganda, and Ethiopia. With a red marker, underline the natural barriers that protected Egypt's ancient civilization. Consult some of the books in your classroom or the Internet for additional information.

CHAPTER 1

BEGINNINGS

When the last great Ice Age ended about twelve thousand years ago, northern Africa looked very different than it does today. Grassy fields and green woodlands covered the plains that are now the arid Sahara Desert. Herds of antelopes and bison, elephants and wild pigs as well as flocks of tropical birds provided early human hunters living there with a plentiful food supply. But over many hundreds of years the climate began to change, and as the terrain gradually dried up and the animals moved on, the people had to look for new sources of food.

The Earliest Nile Dwellers

Between five and seven thousand years ago groups of nomads from northern Africa as well as wanderers from western Asia settled along the banks of the Nile River. The river valley was green and luxuriant, as rich with game and vegetation as the bordering desert was barren. At first the people hunted the animals that came to the river to drink and gathered the fruit and wild grain that grew abundantly along the fertile banks. Each family made its own tools and weapons from stones, animal bones, and the local plants.

In time, the dwellers of the Nile Valley learned that by placing seeds in the soil near the river they could grow their own crops. This discovery probably occurred by accident, when someone dropped some seeds from a basket and then noticed a few days later that they had begun to sprout. But however it took place, this was a major discovery that radically changed the way of

life in Egypt forever. Once the people learned to produce their own crops, they no longer had to wander from place to place in search of food; groups of families could establish permanent villages amid their fields of crops.

The Annual Flood and the Development of Irrigation

The early farmers noticed that every summer the river slowly overflowed its banks and flooded the land as far as the desert border. The heavy spring rains as well as the melting of the snow in the mountains of Ethiopia caused this flooding, but of course the farmers had no idea of its scientific cause. They called the yearly flood the Inundation and considered it an act of the gods. After three months the water would gradually recede, leaving behind a rich deposit of dark silt made of the fine bits of rock and soil washed down from the distant mountains. This silt was a natural fertilizer, and as the water returned to the river bed the farmers eagerly planted their seeds in the rich moist earth.

Unfortunately, the moisture quickly evaporated in the hot desert air and the earth became parched and cracked. It needed moisture. How could the fields be watered in a land where it never rains? The Nile dwellers experimented with ways to keep their soil moist and stumbled upon the basic principles of irrigation. Before long they had developed a highly successful system of watering their crops. Every summer as the flood waters receded, they trapped some of it in small ponds called catch basins. They dug canals to conduct this water to the parts of the fields that were most distant from the river. Other canals were built to conduct water from the river itself. They built dams (of reed matting and mud) and dikes (of wood) to control the flow of the water to the bordering fields. This system provided a supply of water throughout the long dry periods between floods.

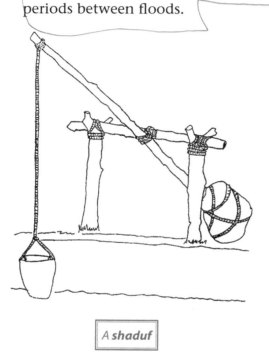

A shaduf

But how could the farmers get the water from the canals onto the fields themselves? At first, they laboriously scooped bucket after bucket by hand. This was back-breaking work, and eventually it was eliminated by an ingenious invention: the *shaduf,* a primitive water pump. This device consisted of a long stick (or small tree) placed horizontally across and tied to two forked sticks that were placed in the ground in a vertical position. To this framework was attached a fourth stick that had a leather bucket tied to a rope on one end and a weight (usually a rock or a clump of dried earth) on the other. The shaduf was

thus a sort of balancing mechanism, like a seesaw. To use it, a farmer simply pulled on the end of the stick with the bucket and lowered it to the level of the water. He dipped the bucket in the water and then released his hold. The weight on the other end of the stick caused the bucket to be lifted up to the level of the field. The farmer then took the bucket and poured the water onto his plants. He repeated this procedure as often as was necessary. The shaduf is still used by Egyptian farmers two thousand years after its invention!

The Black Land and the Red Land

The rich silt deposited by the Nile made its valley the richest farmland in the ancient world. The fields formed narrow strips of vegetation on either side of the river from the First Cataract (the most northern of the series of rapids and waterfalls in the Nile) to the beginning of the delta. The ancient Egyptians referred to the fertile area as the Black Land because of the dark silt. Since in their language *kemi* meant silt, they called their country *Kemet* (the land of the black silt). The ochre colored sand and rock of the desert made up the contrasting Red Land, or *Desret.* Kemet, the Black Land, abounded with life; it was a thriving oasis amid the sterile and bleak stretches of the Red Land. Small wonder that the Egyptians considered their fertile valley the center of the universe!

If you were to fly over Egypt today, you could look down at the thin strips of farmland that flank the Nile as it cuts its way through the desert. Viewed from above, the valley resembles the sinuous body of a green snake, and the delta is its head. The contrast between the rich farmland and the desolate

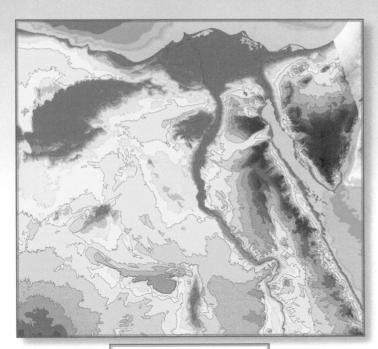

Contrasting terrain of Egypt

it was simply knocked down and a new one was built. Groups of families placed their villages at the edge of the desert, because they wanted to conserve every inch of cultivable soil for their crops. And, of course, they wanted to be safe from the annual floods!

The Domestication of Animals

The early farmers soon discovered the advantages of taming young animals of certain species as a source of food or clothing. They domesticated sheep, goats, donkeys, cattle, geese, and (in the north) pigs. Some of these animals had other uses

desert is striking. So abrupt is the change from one environment to the other that it is possible to stand with one foot in a lush green field and the other in the dry, tawny sand!

← does the nile help even this out?

The soil had uses other than farming for the early Egyptians. They mixed mud from the riverbank with sand or straw and shaped it into bricks, which they then dried in the hot sun. These mud-bricks became the building blocks of their houses. They lasted a long time, since it almost never rains in the Nile Valley. When a wall finally crumbled,

Plowing with domestic oxen.

too. For example, a small group of sheep or goats could be driven across a field to trample and press into the soil the freshly sown seeds. And the inventive farmers soon learned to hitch oxen to a wooden plow.

Other animals were raised for companionship. The Egyptians developed a breed of sleek greyhound dogs and a variety of cat that had long, tufted ears. They also domesticated bees and used the honey to sweeten their food.

A mud-brick house

Donkey carts are still used in Egypt

Major Products

The most important crops were wheat (for making bread), barley (for a kind of beer that became a staple of the daily diet), and flax (a plant whose fibers were used to make linen for clothing). Grapes, cucumbers, dates, onions, lettuce, chickpeas and figs were also cultivated in the fertile soil.

The farmers harvested their wheat with sickles made of wood to which were glued sharp pieces of flint. The wheat cuttings were carried to a warehouse by donkeys. There they were placed in piles on the ground. Cattle were driven over them, trampling the piles and breaking apart the wheat kernels from the tough stalks. Then the women collected the wheat kernels and, using wooden scoops, threw them into the air over and over again; the heavy grain fell to the ground at their feet, while the lighter seed covering (the chaff) drifted away in the breeze. Now the grain could be placed in linen sacks and stored in the warehouse for future use.

Hard work and careful planning eventually made it possible for the early Egyptians to harvest three different crops in a single season, and so there was more than enough food for everyone. As a result, those men who were particularly skilled with their hands could leave the farming to others and devote all of their time to making tools and household items such as pots and vases. This was the beginning of specialization, an important step in the development of a civilization.

The Need for Government

The irrigation projects required the Egyptian farmers to work together cooperatively. Building the dikes and canals was a vast undertaking, and, once dug, the network of waterways had to be inspected and repaired constantly. The neglect of one farmer could imperil the harvest of many families. The need to organize and oversee the irrigation projects led to the creation of local government. At first the older men in a village were in charge. Over the years, as the population

Egyptian farmers, taken from a carving in a tomb

grew and the irrigation projects became more extensive and complex, neighboring villages began to share the management of the canals. It made sense to organize the many ✓ now villages in a local area into a single province. Such a district was called a nome.

how who By 4000 B.C.E. there were many nomes in Egypt, each one ruled by a powerful leader called a nomarch. The nomarch's main responsibilities were to oversee the construction and maintenance of the irrigation system, the storing of surplus grain (and its distribution to the local population in times of famine) and the collection of taxes. The farmers paid their taxes in grain and livestock. There was no currency in Egypt; the economy was based upon barter, the exchange of goods. The collected produce was stored in central warehouses and used to pay the men who helped the nomarch carry out his duties. Those farmers who did not pay their taxes were publicly beaten!

The Kingdoms of Upper Egypt and Lower Egypt

By the year 3300 B.C.E., the nomes lying along the Nile between the First Cataract and the delta were united under one central government led by a powerful monarch. This was called the Kingdom of Upper Egypt because it was upstream from the delta. It had a capital city called Nekheb,

whose patron deity was the vulture goddess Nekhbet. We shall learn more about the gods and goddesses later.

As we have seen, the geography of the delta differs dramatically from that of Upper Egypt. Unlike the narrow valley that dramatically cuts through the sheer limestone cliffs between modern Aswan and Cairo, the delta's small rivulets wander lazily through the low, marshy land of the north. It is here that the river drops its last deposits of silt, and these piles of mud make up hundreds of small islands. The delta is one hundred and twenty-five miles wide at the point where the rivulets finally empty into the Mediterranean Sea. This environment is well suited to fishing, and it is the only part of Egypt where there is sufficient grass for the grazing of large herds of cattle.

Over the years, the people of the delta built walled villages on the dry mounds that rose above the marshes; as in Upper Egypt, these villages were eventually organized into nomes and then ruled by a single monarch. This became the Kingdom of Lower Egypt, so named because it was downstream from the Nile Valley. The capital was Buto, whose patron deity was the cobra goddess Wadjet.

Beginnings of Trade

The Egyptians were an industrious people, and they easily produced a surplus of grain and other crops as well as an abundance of crafts and tools. This led to trade between neighboring villages. An ambitious potter might find a market for his wares a few miles downstream and trade them for tools; an entire village might increase its supply of goats by trading some of its surplus barley. Eventually, merchants began to organize the trading of products up and down the Nile.

Egyptian trade developed rapidly because all the towns and villages were built near the water. The river was a natural highway connecting every community and navigation was a simple affair.

The earliest settlers had fashioned boats out of bundles of reeds of papyrus, a plant that grew along the river banks, particularly in the delta. These vessels were light and buoyant, bouncing gently over the waves of the river. Later, more substantial boats were made from the wood of local palm trees. A linen sail attached to a pole would catch the wind, making a boat even more navigable.

Drawing of an Egyptian boat

Since the prevailing winds along the Nile come from the Mediterranean to the north, and the current, of course, flows from the south, the Egyptians could easily travel along the river in either direction: They caught the wind with their sails to go south or simply drifted with the current moving north (the later addition of oars gave them extra speed in this direction). It is not surprising that the two Egyptian words for travel were *khent* (meaning "to go upstream") and *khed* ("to go downstream").

The alternative to travel along the river was considerably less attractive. The dirt roads that bordered the fields were deeply rutted, and they were under water part of the year. Furthermore, traveling by donkey cart was awkward and uncomfortable when compared with riding on a boat.

Trade was actively carried on between the peoples of Upper and Lower Egypt. The major products of the delta were onions, lettuce, watermelons, leather tanned from the hides of the cattle, and the papyrus plant, which grew so abundantly in the marshes. The desert hills bordering the valley of Upper Egypt provided the limestone, sandstone, and granite needed for official building projects as well as alabaster and basalt for making statues and vases.

Trade was not limited to the villages along the Nile, however. Because of their proximity to the Mediterranean (which the Egyptians called the "Great Green Sea"), the people of Lower Egypt had contact with merchants from Asia and Crete. Dwellers of Upper Egypt occasionally traded with foreigners residing south of the First Cataract.

Despite their interaction brought about through trade, the cultures of Lower and Upper Egypt were distinctly different.

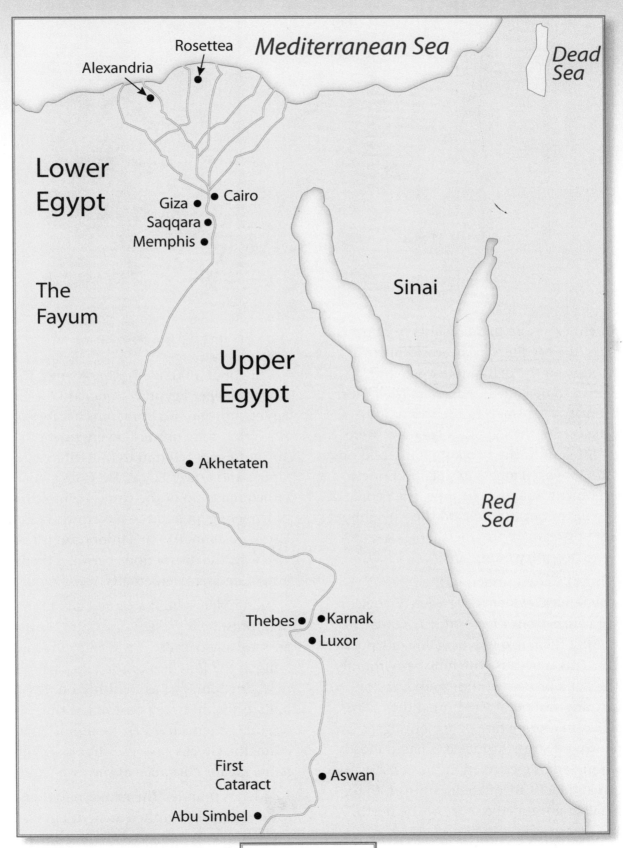

Rosettea

Alexandria

Mediterranean Sea

Dead Sea

Lower Egypt

Giza

Cairo

Saqqara

Memphis

The Fayum

Sinai

Upper Egypt

Akhetaten

Red Sea

Thebes

Karnak

Luxor

First Cataract

Aswan

Abu Simbel

Upper and Lower Egypt

Carving of pharaoh wearing double crown

Frequent exposure to merchants from other parts of the Mediterranean world made the people of the delta more open and receptive to new ideas than were their more conservative kinsmen in the south. Even the dialects of the Egyptian language were very different in the two kingdoms, and one could always tell a person's place of origin the moment he spoke. In time, the people of Lower Egypt began to regard their neighbors living upstream as provincial and close-minded "country bumpkins."

Unfortunately, much of the archaeological evidence we have of ancient Egypt comes from the hot desert sands bordering the narrow river valley of Upper Egypt. This is because the moist environment of the delta promoted the rapid decay of nearly anything that was buried there. For this reason, our picture of ancient Egypt is somewhat distorted, since it is based mostly upon materials recovered in the conservative south and lacks adequate input from the more liberal-minded culture of the north.

Two Kingdoms Become One

In about 3100 B.C.E. King Menes, the ruler of Upper Egypt, conquered Lower Egypt, and the two kingdoms became one. From that time onward, every ruler of ancient Egypt referred to himself as King of Upper and Lower Egypt. He wore a double crown made up of the conical white crown of Upper Egypt and the red crown of Lower Egypt to symbolize this important union. In this way, the distinctions between the two kingdoms were perpetually acknowledged.

King Menes built a capital city at Memphis, near present day Cairo. This was an ideal site because it was centrally located, lying at the junction of the two parts of his new kingdom, just as Washington, D.C. was built at the midway point of the thirteen original American states. Memphis is the name the Greeks gave the city; its Egyptian name means, "Balance of the Two Lands."

Menes founded the first dynasty, or royal family, of a united ancient Egypt. Thirty more dynasties (including 330 kings) were to follow. Menes was killed one day when he was wounded by a hippopotamus while hunting in the delta. However, the unification of the two kingdoms had been firmly established, and it would endure for a very long time.

Questions

1. What was northern Africa like at the end of the last great Ice Age?

2. What caused the annual flooding of the Nile?

3. Describe a shaduf and explain how it was used.

4. What were the Black Land and the Red Land?

5. Where did the Egyptians build their villages?

6. How did the Egyptians use the animals they domesticated?

7. What is specialization of labor?

8. How did the use of irrigation lead to the creation of a system of government?

9. Why is Upper Egypt located below Lower Egypt on a map?

10. What do you know about Menes?

Further Thoughts

1. Throughout their history, the Egyptians recognized that their civilization could not exist without the rich bounties of nature. They depended upon the constancy of a bright blue cloudless sky in the daytime and gentle, cool breezes in the evening. A storm was a rare occurrence, except near the Mediterranean Sea. The Nile flooded its banks and then receded back into its bed with dependable regularity. As long as the farmers worked hard in their fields and maintained the canals and dikes, they were almost always rewarded with a rich harvest.

It is not surprising, therefore, that the ancient Egyptians believed that regularity and repetition of a pattern were essential parts of a good life. Change threw them off balance and made them very uncomfortable. This was, of course, particularly true in Upper Egypt. Following tradition, which meant doing everything the way it had always been done, was of critical importance. This Egyptian penchant for routine and the familiar helps to explain why the civilization that evolved after the time of Menes changed so little over a period of nearly three thousand years.

2. The names of Upper and Lower Egypt can be confusing when you look at a map, because Upper Egypt appears at the bottom and Lower Egypt is at the top! This problem can be solved by remembering that the Nile flows downward from the mountains (high up) until it reaches sea level (down low).

Drawing of one side of the palette.

3. Most scholars agree that Menes was also known as Narmer. He was a fierce warrior. The two pictures of him that exist today were carved on a ceremonial palette used for mixing eye paint. In one, he is smashing the skull of a wounded adversary with a heavy club; in the other, he is marching in front of piles of the headless bodies of his vanquished enemies!

4. Sometimes a farmer flailed his wheat crop with an instrument consisting of a handle with a few freely swinging strips of leather attached to one end. This manual thresher would cause the grain to fall to the ground. As we shall see, the flail later became a symbol of might and authority.

Projects

1. Make a relief map of Egypt and its southern neighbors out of clay or instant paper maché. Show how the Nile originates in the lowlands of Uganda (the White Nile) and the mountains of Ethiopia (the Blue Nile) and then travels to the Mediterranean Sea. Use aluminum foil or varnish to make the river bed and valley waterproof. Then pour water into the sources of the river to reenact the Inundation.

2. Make a shaduf, using whatever materials are available to you. One suggestion is to use popsicle sticks, a plastic cup and a stone, or you can try to make a life-sized model using branches, a bucket and some sort of weight.

3. The papyrus plant was one of Egypt's most versatile products. Make a poster showing papyrus growing in the delta and then draw illustrations of the various ways in which the plant was used. Some examples are paper, sandals, and boats; there are many more uses. Look at the illustrations in the books in your classroom for ideas.

4. Today there are many *feluccas* in the Nile. Find out what they are, and draw a picture of one of them.

CHAPTER 2

THE PHARAOH

The king of Egypt became known as the pharaoh. This title has an interesting derivation. Perhaps for superstitious reasons, the ancient Egyptians considered it improper to address their king by name. Therefore, his subjects referred to him in a more roundabout way. Since the king lived in a very large and grand house, translated as *per aa* in Egyptian, they adopted the word *pharaoh*, which means "he who lives in the great house." Such an indirect term of address is still used today when newscasters report about the latest remarks made by "the White House," referring, of course, to the President who lives there.

The King's Titles

The pharaoh had two names and at least five titles, which were recited at religious ceremonies and written on tombs and official documents. His first name was the one he bore as a prince, such as Ramses or Seti, and it is the one by which historians know him. He also had a throne name, such as Menkheperre (which means "enduring like the forms of the god Ra"). Since these names were considered too sacred to be written as ordinary words, they were enclosed in an oval ring (later called a cartouche) to separate them from other secular words. To the left of the cartouche were written the symbols meaning "the King of Upper and Lower Egypt." The pharaoh's other titles included "Horus" (the name of a god), "Lord of the Diadem of the Vulture and of the Snake" (remember the patron deities of the capital cities of the two kingdoms?), "the Son of Ra," "the Sedge and Bee," and "the Golden Horus." Over the years, even more titles were added, so that the full address of a pharaoh would make a rather long paragraph or require several minutes to recite!

The people believed that the pharaoh was descended from the gods, and so his commands were never questioned. In fact, it was considered sinful to disobey him; anyone arrogant (or foolish) enough to dispute his word could have his ears chopped off! Because of his divine status, the pharaoh could supposedly interpret the will of the gods. He was the high priest of the land, and his main duty was to appeal through religious rites to the deities responsible for such important natural events as the shining of the sun, the flooding of the Nile and the coming of spring.

The pharaoh

The pharaoh was also responsible for maintaining order throughout his kingdom. He regulated the labor of the farmers, oversaw the building and maintenance of irrigation projects, and coordinated the collection of taxes. He was the chief justice, the ultimate judge in all disputes that occurred throughout Egypt. Justice in those days was translated as "what the pharaoh loves" and wrongdoing was simply "what the pharaoh hates."

The Childhood of the Pharaoh

The pharaoh passed on his title and position to the oldest son of his first wife. (Every pharaoh had many wives.) As a child, the heir apparent had a pleasant life, playing with his brothers and sisters in the warm sunshine. His head would be shaven except for a single long side lock, and like all very young Egyptians he would usually run about naked. At the age of eight or nine he was tutored in reading, writing and mathematics. His brothers shared in this education, since there was always the possibility that the oldest boy would die. Should that happen, the next oldest son took his place. The boys also learned to hunt and to perform in military tournaments.

While still a child, the prince would be married to a sister or cousin (usually the eldest daughter of the reigning pharaoh). Royal marriages always took place within the family, for the Egyptians wanted to keep the blood pure! A major exception to this rule was Pepi I, who had a non-royal wife. The pharaoh would have many other wives, but his first wife would always be the most important, and her oldest son would automatically inherit the crown after his death.

Marrying one's own sister or cousin is a tradition that seems strange to us. But it is important to remember that there were many royal children, since the king had many wives. For example, King Ramses II had over one hundred offspring! By the age of eight or nine, the boys lived apart from the girls, and so the siblings and half-siblings hardly knew each other, if at all. So marrying someone from the royal household probably seemed like marrying someone from the same town, rather than a brother or sister.

The Power of the Pharaoh

Everything in the kingdom belonged to the pharaoh. He owned the land, the crops, the animals, and the very souls of his subjects. Hundreds of thousands of farmers toiled in the fields to serve him. In return, he made certain that the gods produced the annual flood and a good harvest, that the sun rose each morning and that the people were protected from natural disasters and attacks from foreign predators. Belief in the great power of the pharaoh gave the Egyptian people a sense of security. The weather that was always sunny and dry, the flood that happened every year, and the natural barriers that protected the valley made it easy for the pharaoh to keep his promises. As long as their lives were predictable, the people were content and their civilization flourished.

Although the earliest pharaohs attempted to perform all duties themselves, it soon became clear that one man could not manage everything in Egyptian society. And so, early on each new pharaoh delegated some of his duties to his relatives and the heads of the most important families of the nation. He had a sort of prime minister, called a vizier, who was second in command. The vizier handled the everyday matters that came up, oversaw the public works, and advised the pharaoh on important matters of state. Later there were two viziers, one to represent each of the two kingdoms of Upper and Lower Egypt. There was also a chancellor who collected taxes. Scribes kept account of all business and government transactions. Eventually, a government network came into being—every town, city and province had officials who managed local affairs and reported to the pharaoh and his circle of ministers in the capital city.

As we shall see, in the later periods of Egyptian history the pharaoh waged war and declared peace. When the valley nation expanded into an empire, his attention was often directed toward distant lands and away from his own people. He became a warrior god.

Many pharaohs ruled over Egypt during the three thousand years of its civilization. Some were good, some were bad, but very few were assassinated or deprived of office. The people accepted the word of a newly crowned pharaoh when he swore to be a good ruler, to care for the helpless, to prevent bribery and fight oppression, to treat all men equally, to promote justice, and to utter no evil. The longest reign was that of Pepi II. He came to the throne when he was six and was still pharaoh ninety-four years later at the age of one hundred!

A lofty image, the pharaoh sat upon a wooden throne when he performed his duties as chief justice. Everyone was required to kneel in front of him and to kiss the dust about his feet. A privileged few were allowed to actually kiss the ruler's feet! After an audience, a subject was expected to back out of the throne room with his eyes cast downwards. The pharaoh usually wore the double crown of Lower and Upper Egypt. Sometimes, when there was a conflict over territory, he wore the war crown (the *kepresh*). This was made of blue leather studded with golden sequins, and above his brow was the *uraeus*, the brightly colored cobra goddess spitting fire at the enemies of Egypt. On less formal occasions he wore a *nemes*, a cloth headdress woven of linen and gold threads. The two sides of the *nemes* fell over his shoulders in pleats.

Flail and crook.

In his hands the pharaoh held a crook and a flail, objects symbolic of his power. The Egyptians thought of their ruler as a good shepherd, carrying a crook to gently guide his flocks (his subjects). He carried a flail (a kind of whip) to defend his people against an enemy. The flail also implied that the pharaoh would punish those who did not obey his commandments.

The Egyptians shaved their bodies as well as their heads, so the pharaoh wore a false beard, attached by a strap that tied at the back of his head. His only clothing in the

Pharaoh Tutankamon, coffin portrait

Despite his luxurious life style, the pharaoh must have been a lonely figure. Although he had his government officials to carry out his orders, he was held responsible for the smooth running of the national economy, the welfare of his people, and the satisfaction of the gods. That was no small task.

Questions

1. What does the word "pharaoh" mean?
2. Why was it considered sinful to disobey the pharaoh?
3. What were the pharaoh's duties?
4. Why did a bureaucracy of government develop in Egypt?
5. Describe the attire of the pharaoh as he sat upon the throne.

Further Thoughts

1. Egypt was the first civilization to have a complex government bureaucracy. Our own system of federalism (three levels of government: central, state and local) owes much to the men who organized the cities and towns in Egypt over five thousand years ago.

2. After a pharaoh had ruled for thirty years, a special jubilee festival, called the *Heb Sed*, was celebrated. Its purpose was to thank the gods for the good works of the monarch. The highlight of the festival was a ritual race in which the pharaoh ran around a circular course in the hot sun. The object of the race was to renew his strength and to grant him a long life, but it must have been a difficult feat for an aging monarch who routinely got very little exercise!

hot, dry climate of Egypt was a white linen skirt. In very early times a lion's tail was attached to the back, another symbol of his regal status. He wore elaborate jewelry made of gold and precious stones: a wide collar called a pectoral, bracelets, rings and even earrings (his ears were pierced). Standard royal footwear was leather sandals.

When the pharaoh traveled, he often rode in a litter (a wooden throne mounted on poles and carried on the shoulders of slaves). Beside him fan-bearers waved fans of ostrich plumes or woven fibers to keep him cool, while other servants shook bouquets of flowers near his head, filling the air about his royal presence with a sweet perfume.

Projects:

1. Draw a picture of a pharaoh seated upon his throne. Choose any headdress you prefer, but be sure to include the crook and flail. Check the illustrations in several books in your library or classroom or on sites on the internet before you begin.

2. Write a short play about a peasant who comes to see the pharaoh to complain about something that has happened in his village. Select some friends to help you present the play to the class.

3. Find the names of all the pharaohs of Egypt. On a poster board make a time line showing the reigns of the rulers, arranging them according to dynasties.

4. Compare the duties of the pharaoh with those of a modern American president. Who has the more difficult job? Write a short paper giving reasons for your opinion.

CHAPTER 3

THE THREE GREAT PERIODS OF EGYPTIAN HISTORY

The history of ancient Egypt following Menes' unification of the two lands is usually divided into three major time periods. These are known as the Old Kingdom, the Middle Kingdom, and the New Kingdom. Each of these rich and productive eras lasted hundreds of years, and each came to an end because of civil war, national disaster, or invasion by foreign armies.

This chapter presents an overview of the major events of each period. Later chapters will describe in greater detail the religion, writing, art, architecture, math, science, and daily life of ancient Egyptian civilization.

THE OLD KINGDOM C. 2700-2200 B.C.E.: THE AGE OF THE PYRAMIDS

A Powerful Central Government

During the Old Kingdom, the Egyptian nation grew from a collection of loosely organized farming villages into an extensive network of cities and towns. The pharaoh and his advisors in Memphis presided over a tightly knit bureaucracy (a system of departments or bureaus) that affected nearly every aspect of the lives of the people. This was history's first great centralized government.

Egypt's unique geography was a key factor in the development of this highly organized state, since it was rather easy for top-ranking officials to keep tabs on the activities of the long string of communities that lined the single central highway, the Nile. The divine status of the pharaoh further guaranteed the obedience of the people; to dispute his word was unthinkable! Stone statues carved during the Old Kingdom show the pharaoh as a lofty figure, serenely confident of his absolute power over his subjects.

New Professions

The efficient irrigation system developed in earlier times produced bountiful harvests. Apart from an occasional lean year when the level of the Inundation was below average, the people had more than enough to eat. The rich harvests of wheat and barley offered proof that hard labor under the blazing sun was worthwhile, and so the peasants who made up the majority of the population toiled diligently and complained very little. At the same time, the prospering economy made it possible for a growing number of men to specialize in activities other than farming. Some spent their time building or inspecting the canals while others were hunters and fishermen. Those with a more creative bent became shipbuilders, architects, artists and priests.

New Horizons

Over the years, trade expanded to an international level as, timidly and cautiously,

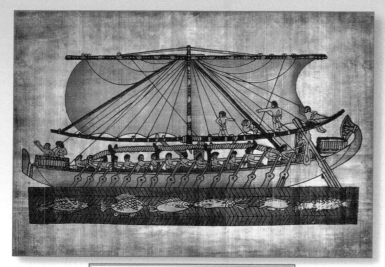

Ancient painting of an Egyptian ship

Egyptian sailors ventured beyond the gently flowing Nile into the more turbulent waters of the Mediterranean and the Red Sea. They hugged the coast since they had no navigational devices and they were terrified of the open waters. Their wide-beamed vessels were loaded with linen, pottery, stone vases, statues, and jewelry. They journeyed eastward and then north to Byblos (a city in modern day Lebanon) to obtain cedar; this hard and attractive wood was needed by Egyptian builders for the construction of boats as well as the roofs of temples and palaces. They docked further north in Syrian ports to trade with merchants for lapis lazuli, a beautiful blue stone used to adorn jewelry.

Egyptian seamen also ventured up the Nile to Nubia (modern Sudan); they had to beach their boats at the cataracts and laboriously carry them upstream until the water became navigable once again. From the Nubians they obtained such luxury items as gold, ebony, ivory and panther skins. They also bargained for slaves. Gold, however, was Nubia's greatest resource; in fact, Nubia means "gold" in Egyptian.

Egypt Enters The Copper Age

About this time, there were many tribes from Asia living in Sinai. They mined the local copper and transported it to cities on the Mediterranean coast. This metal could be melted down and shaped into tools and weapons that were vastly superior to the more primitive stone implements used in the Nile Valley. It could also be fashioned into practical household items like cups and plates. The large shipments of copper that were brought back to Egypt on merchant ships led to a thriving new industry among the local craftsmen. Sinai was also the source of beautiful turquoise stones, and these were much sought after by Egyptian jewelers.

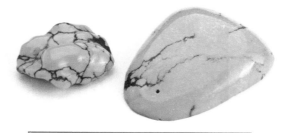

Turquoise in its rough and finished form

Toward the end of the Old Kingdom, Pharaoh Pepi I drove the local tribesmen out of Sinai and made the entire peninsula a part of Egypt. From then on, Egyptian artisans had an unlimited and cheap supply of copper and turquoise.

The Egyptians' Distrust of Foreigners

Despite the expansion of trade, Egypt remained in many ways an isolated society throughout the Old Kingdom. Most Egyptians were suspicious of foreigners,

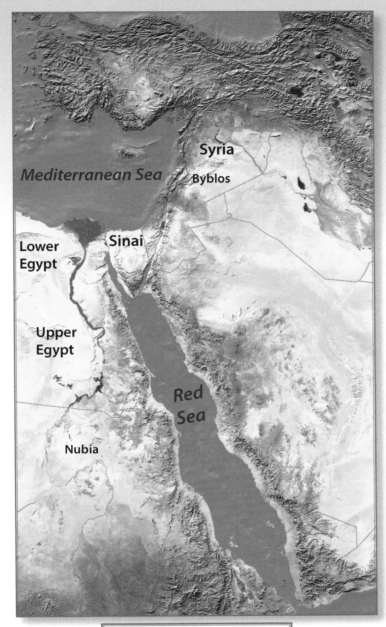

The Eastern Mediterranean World

cultures was based upon the reports of soldiers and merchants. These accounts were probably distorted and exaggerated as they were passed on from person to person. (Just think about how modern rumors are spread.) In any event, Egypt was very much a nation of conservative, stay-at-home people who avoided the new and the unfamiliar whenever possible.

The Concept of Writing Arrives From the Middle East

On rare occasions, however, foreign innovations did make their way into the Nile Valley. The most important example of this is writing. The concept of drawing symbols to represent ideas came from Mesopotamia (modern Iraq), where a rich civilization known as Sumer flourished as early as the fourth millennium B.C.E. The Sumerians invented a kind of writing called cuneiform, which we will learn more about later. People from Mesopotamia might have been among the early settlers of Egypt, and later on Egyptian merchants dealt with merchants from that region. So, one way or another, cuneiform became known to the Egyptians; they, in turn, experimented with the idea of writing, and by the time of the Old Kingdom they had created their own written language using symbols known as hieroglyphs.

Construction of the Pyramids

By 2600 B.C.E. the Egyptians had mastered many basic concepts in mathematics, geometry and science; this knowledge, combined with the tight organization and discipline of their society, enabled them to build huge stone

whose customs and outward appearance were so different from their own. They believed that the fertile strip of land bordering the Nile was the center of the earth, created for them by the gods; for this reason, everyone living beyond Egyptian boundaries occupied an inferior status in their eyes. Of course, the vast majority of Egyptian people never traveled more than a few miles beyond the town where they were born, and their knowledge of foreign

Pyramids at Giza

monuments called pyramids (some were over five hundred feet high!). These massive structures were so well engineered that many of them still exist today, five thousand years after they were built. We will learn more about the pyramids in Chapter VII.

Decline of the Old Kingdom

Because of the many achievements of the Old Kingdom in architecture, mathematics and science, this period is considered an intellectual high point of Egyptian civilization, a standard by which later accomplishments are measured.

All good things must come to an end, however, and the Old Kingdom began its decline during the sixth dynasty. There were a number of factors that weakened the Egyptian state. First, a vast amount of the royal treasury was spent on the building and maintenance of pyramids and the temples associated with them. And while the treasury was being drained in this manner, many members of the upper classes found loopholes in the tax laws that enabled them to avoid paying their fair share. The opportunities for this were many. For example, greedy landowners (including the priests) often avoided paying any taxes at all by simply registering newly acquired estates in the name of a god or of a dead ancestor. Unfortunately, the government could not supervise the taxation of all the people, so while the pharaoh's vast treasury diminished, the priests and nobles became immensely rich!

As the population of Egypt grew, the pharaoh was forced to delegate more and more of his power to the nobles and government officials. At the same time, the nomarchs began to seek more independence. Since the days of Menes, the pharaoh had appointed these provincial governors, but in the waning years of the Old Kingdom titles began to be passed on from father to son. Since the new nomarchs no longer depended upon the pharaoh for their power, they displayed an arrogance that would have been unthinkable in earlier times. The power of Egypt's king was rapidly dwindling, and he could no longer keep all the promises he made to his people.

The End of Order

The last pharaoh of the Old Kingdom was Pepi II. Although his reign lasted for an incredible ninety years, government officials were actually in power much of the time—during his childhood and again during the long period of his old age. Sadly, these men were more interested in amassing their own personal wealth than preserving the stability of the nation. When Pepi finally died, the central government fell completely apart. During the twenty years following Pepi's death, there were twenty pharaohs; none of them could put things back together again.

Egypt gradually returned to the primitive state it had been before Menes. The nomes that had been administrative centers at the start of the Old Kingdom became independent states once again. These were often at war with one another, as each nomarch tried to increase his power and influence over his neighbors.

The final blow to what remained of the Old Kingdom was a famine. The Nile did not flood its banks with its usual volume of water for several years. As a result, the harvests were small and many people starved. There is at least one account of cannibalism. It seemed as though the peace and prosperity of the last five hundred years were gone forever. In the writings of the time appear these gloomy words: "every good thing has disappeared."

Because the light of learning and intellectual fervor seemed to have gone out, the period following the dissolution of the Old Kingdom is known as the Dark Ages of ancient Egypt.

THE MIDDLE KINGDOM C. 2000-1700 B.C.E.: AN AGE OF PROSPERITY

Egypt Is Reunited

After years of civil wars, Mentuhotep, the ruler of the city of Thebes in Upper Egypt, successfully led his army up and down the Nile against the feuding nomarchs and won control of the entire nation. At last order was reestablished in Egypt. Thebes replaced Memphis as the capital city. After the rather brief reign of two Theban pharaohs, a new dynasty was founded (the 12th); this family would rule over Egypt for the remainder of the Middle Kingdom.

The anarchy of the final years of the Old Kingdom had made it clear that Egypt needed a very strong central government. The monarchs of the 12th Dynasty saw to it that the power of the nomarchs was quietly whittled away. The nobles would never again challenge the authority of the pharaoh.

A Greater Sharing of the Wealth

With the return of prosperity, Egypt's middle class of traders, scribes and craftsmen rapidly expanded. These enterprising

individuals greatly enriched the artistic and intellectual life of Egyptian society. In fact, craftsmen of the Middle Kingdom created the most beautiful jewelry ever seen in Egypt, and a new class of writers produced a wealth of poetry, myths and legends, making this a golden age of literature.

The middle class of this period developed a taste for luxury items that were formerly available only to the pharaohs and the nobility. Trade expanded as merchants sought the gold and silver trinkets and the ostrich plumes that were becoming "all the rage."

With the growing demand for more comfortable life styles came a waning interest in impressive tombs for the hereafter. The pyramids of this period were built of mudbrick, not stone, and they were shoddy and vastly inferior to the majestic monuments of the Old Kingdom. But, on balance, it was probably a good thing that less was spent on

A turquoise medallion

the tombs of the royal family and nobles and more funds were available for public projects.

The Conquest of Nubia

The greatest pharaoh of the 12th Dynasty was Senwosnet. Early in his reign he ordered a channel 250 feet long and 34 feet wide cut through the granite rocks beside the rapids of the First Cataract. This bypass enabled his war galleys to sail directly into Nubia, which was easily conquered and made part of Egypt's territory. All the gold in the Nubian mines became a part of Egypt's national wealth.

Senwosnet later extended the Egyptian frontier further upstream to the Third Cataract, 450 miles south of modern Aswan. He built a fortified town (Buhen) on the Nubian border from which his army could oversee the mining of the gold and control the trade route into the African continent. In time, a series of stone fortresses with crenellated battlements and moveable drawbridges were built along the Nubian frontier to protect Egyptian interests. The basic design of the imposing castles that we associate with the knights of the Middle Ages can be traced back to these ancient fortresses.

The Search for New Markets

As the economy prospered, the Nile valley and the delta produced a huge surplus of flax and linen, papyrus, salted fish, ox hides, alabaster, and many crafts, and so the Egyptian merchants looked for new customers. Caravans of men and donkeys frequently made an eight-day trek across the eastern desert to the Red Sea. It was a difficult journey, for the men had to carry

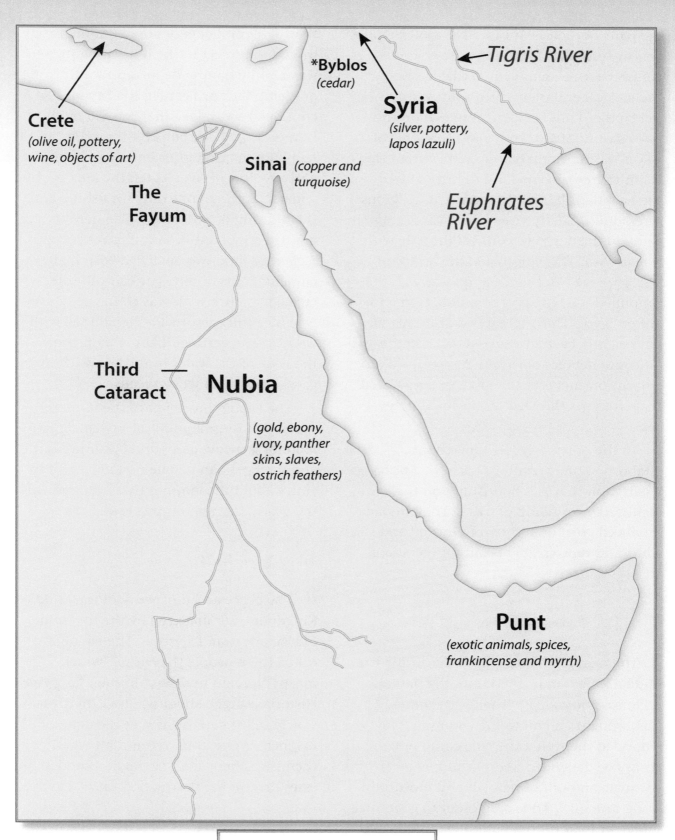

Crete
(olive oil, pottery,
wine, objects of art)

The
Fayum

*Byblos
(cedar)

Syria
(silver, pottery,
lapos lazuli)

Sinai (copper and
turquoise)

Tigris River

*Euphrates
River*

Third
Cataract

Nubia

(gold, ebony,
ivory, panther
skins, slaves,
ostrich feathers)

Punt
(exotic animals, spices,
frankincense and myrrh)

Trading Centers of the Middle Kingdom

the parts of their boat as well as food supplies and the products they wished to trade. The vessels were reassembled on the coast of the Red Sea and then sailed southward to the land of Punt (modern Somalia) on the east coast of Africa. Punt was the source of spices, exotic animals and such fragrant tree resins as frankincense and myrrh (which the Egyptians burned as incense in religious ceremonies). Many years later a canal was cut through the desert to connect the Nile with the Red Sea. This eliminated the awkward trek across the hot sands and greatly simplified the transport of products in and out of Egypt. The original bed of this canal has recently been discovered beneath the sand and pebbles of eastern Egypt. It was an ancient precursor to the modern Suez Canal that connects the Mediterranean and Red Seas.

To the north, Egyptian merchants established trade relations with the Minoan civilization that was flourishing on the Mediterranean island of Crete. The Minoans produced great quantities of olive oil and wine, and they created beautiful objects of art.

The Draining of the Fayum

The men of science who lived during the Middle Kingdom learned from the natural calamities of the past. The great famine that brought an end to the Old Kingdom reminded them that the Nile could not always be depended upon to supply an adequate amount of new silt and moisture along its banks. And so, in order to guarantee sufficient food for the nation when the level of the Inundation was low, the Egyptian engineers of the Middle Kingdom focused

their skills and energies on an immense irrigation project in the fertile Fayum, a 670 square mile natural depression southwest of Memphis. Eons earlier, the Fayum had contained a vast lake that was fed by the waters of the Nile, but over the centuries silt had built up around its entrance. Deprived of a steady flow of river water, the area became a marshland, suitable only for fishing and the hunting of water fowl. The new project drained about ten thousand acres and this reclaimed land was encircled with high embankments of dirt. The run-off water created a new lake. It was connected to the Nile by a thirty foot wide canal lined with wooden and earthen dikes. A dam controlled the level of the water in the lake with sluice gates made from woven reeds.

The Fayum project gave the farmers access to a huge amount of extremely fertile land for growing crops and pasturing cattle, and the Egyptian people no longer had to worry about the famines that occurred when the yearly Inundation was low.

Invasion by the Hyksos

The peace and prosperity of the Middle Kingdom were shattered by the invasion of nomads from Palestine. The Egyptians called these people the *Hyksos*, which means "foreign invaders" in their language. Historians argue about whether the Hyksos slowly infiltrated the area of the delta or invaded in one swift assault. But whether their invasion was a gradual or a sudden one, it resulted in the destruction of the Egyptian state.

The invaders had no trouble defeating the pharaoh's troops, because their army had the advantage of the latest advance in military technology: the horse and chariot. Each chariot had two wheels and carried two soldiers: one man controlled the horse or horses while the other either shot arrows from a high velocity composite bow or hurled bronze-tipped spears. (Bronze is a metal made by melting copper and tin.) The pharaoh's army was made up of foot-soldiers carrying primitive spears and arrows that were tipped with copper, a metal far softer than bronze, and the only wheeled vehicles in Egypt were vegetable carts pulled by donkeys!

The Egyptian soldiers were no match for the foreign charioteers. In time, the Hyksos took over the delta and established their own nation there; the Egyptians living in Lower Egypt thus became the unwilling subjects of their conquerors. The Hyksos did not settle in Upper Egypt, but the provinces there were forced to pay an annual tribute of gold and jewelry. The new rulers also formed an alliance with Kush, the northern part of Nubia, which was now ruled by local princes.

A lute

Contributions of the Conquerors

The influence of the Hyksos was not completely harmful, since they made a number of useful contributions to Egyptian culture. For example, they introduced the upright loom, a mechanism that greatly improved the quality of woven Egyptian linen. They imported such musical instruments as the lute, the lyre, the oboe and the tambourine, and these were later used to play Egyptian melodies. They introduced the concept of the potter's wheel. And they brought in strong and tractable hump-backed cattle from Asia to plow the fields. Perhaps their greatest contribution was the technology of melting down copper and tin to produce bronze.

But despite the many innovations brought by the Hyksos, the Egyptians always resented their occupation. In fact, the very presence of these outsiders on Egyptian soil was considered intolerable great humiliation.

THE NEW KINGDOM C. 1500-1000 B.C.E.: THE EGYPTIAN EMPIRE

New Weapons

After years of subjugation, the Egyptians finally threw off their shackles and regained independence. They were able to do this by mastering the technology of their oppressors. They learned to mold durable weapons and shields of bronze. They copied the design of the composite bow and the battle ax that the Hyksos had used so effectively against them, and they also experimented with chain armor. But their greatest accomplishment was to produce war chariots that were lighter and more maneuverable than those of the Hyksos. Each chariot was manned by a driver holding a whip and the reins and a fighter armed with a composite bow.

The Invaders Are Finally Driven Out

When the time was ripe, Sequenenra, a prince from Thebes, organized a powerful army and led it against the Hyksos soldiers garrisoned in the delta. Terrible ax wounds on his mummy indicate that Sequenenra was killed in battle; it was left to his son and successor, Kamose, to drive the Hyksos out of Egypt. Kamose was succeeded by his brother Ahmose, who pursued the Hyksos into Palestine where he annihilated their army. Once back in Egypt, he reunited the Upper and Lower Kingdoms and reestablished the power of the central government. He reclaimed Nubia by driving out the local princes who had been ruling there during the Hyksos' occupation. The fortresses built in earlier times were repaired and enlarged, and new ones were constructed. Egypt was once again a unified state. Ahmose founded the powerful 18th Dynasty that would rule for centuries.

A New Spirit

An aggressive spirit not seen in earlier times defined the New Kingdom. Just as the decline of the Old Kingdom had taught the Egyptians the importance of maintaining a strong central leadership, the invasion of the Hyksos made it clear that they could no longer depend upon the natural barriers surrounding their nation to keep out foreign armies. The days of peaceful self-sufficiency in the delta and Nile valley were now past. In the new age, the Egyptians would become active aggressors who conquered the peoples living near their borders in order to create a buffer zone against any unexpected attack. In the process, Egypt would become very rich. In fact, during the New Kingdom Egypt reached the peak of its prosperity as well as the pinnacle of its power.

The pharaohs of the New Kingdom, unlike their predecessors, took an active part in military campaigns. Dressed in bronze and leather body armor, they personally led their chariot squadrons into battle. No longer regarded as serene and lofty interpreters of the messages of the gods, they became courageous warriors.

Thutmose I

Thutmose I was the next pharaoh of distinction to rule. His conquest of Syria made Egypt the first imperial power ever to

Tomb painting of a pharaoh in a war chariot. In reality, there would also have been a driver.

rule in western Asia. He also campaigned in Nubia, pushing Egypt's borders further south to the Fourth Cataract. Thutmose built many temples, and he was the first pharaoh to be buried in the rugged cliffs rising one thousand feet above the Nile opposite Thebes. This bleak burial ground came to be known as the Valley of the Kings. We shall learn more about the royal cemeteries in a later chapter.

The son of Thutmose (Thutmose II) was a sickly youth. He married his sister (or cousin) Hatshepsut, and after a few years he died. Since he and Hatshepsut had no sons, Thutmose II was succeeded by the six-year-old son of one of his other wives. The boy was named Thutmose III. The events of his early years make an interesting tale.

Egypt's First Great Woman Leader

At first, Hatshepsut was willing to remain in the background as the young boy assumed the title of pharaoh. However, she slowly gained influence among the government officials who were actually running the country, and before long she was making many important decisions of state. She claimed that she was entitled to this authority because she was the regent of her stepson. Hatshepsut was a determined woman. A scribe once described her as a "raging crocodile," since she was determined to always have her way in matters of state.

Hatshepsut became so powerful that she was able to have the young king sent off to a temple to study with the priests. Once he was out of the way, she declared herself the rightful pharaoh of Egypt. This was a revolutionary idea in a society that had always been ruled by men, but Hatshepsut was highly intelligent and ambitious. She became history's first great woman leader.

Not that she appeared feminine. For official ceremonies she donned the garb of a male pharaoh, including the false beard. And so it is not surprising that the writings of the time reveal some confusion about the proper way of addressing the Egyptian leader: Hatshepsut was alternately referred to as His Majesty and Her Majesty!

Hatshepsut ruled effectively as pharaoh for twenty years, with the aid of her chief minister and temple architect, Senmut. She had little interest in extending the

Statue of Hatshepsut dressed as the pharaoh

boundaries of the Egyptian empire. Rather, she focused her energies upon expanding trade, and she sent many ships to Nubia for such luxury items as ostrich plumes and leopard skins as well as for slaves. She also sent a fleet of five vessels to the land of Punt, modern Ethiopia. They returned to Egypt with ebony, ivory, gold, monkeys, greyhounds, a giraffe, and thirty-one living myrrh trees. Hatshepsut directed the beautification of the city of Thebes, and she commissioned the building of a magnificent tomb and mortuary temple for her next life at Deir el Bahri in the Valley of the Queens (which is where the myrrh trees were planted). There is a photograph of her temple in Chapter 7. She also used the nation's vast wealth to repair the temples up and down the Nile that had been damaged by the Hyksos.

Thutmose III Seeks Revenge

Hatshepsut's reign was one of peace and prosperity. It was a good time for all Egyptians, but the young Thutmose III had grown into manhood and he could not be held off indefinitely. Finally, he stormed into the palace and demanded his title. Before long, Hatshepsut was dead. Did she die a natural death, or did Thutmose have her murdered? We will never know precisely what happened, but we do know that after her demise Thutmose sought to erase every trace of the woman who had usurped his power for so long. He had her name chiseled from carvings on the stone surfaces of her temple and wherever it appeared upon other monuments, often replacing it with his own. This was a major offense to Hatshepsut, since the Egyptians believed that destroying every record of a person's name would deny him (or her) of immortality. Thutmose ordered Hatshepsut's statues to be smashed and thrown into deep pits. Ironically, by so

Carved painting of Thutmose (right) and the god Amon.

doing he actually caused the remnants of her statues (and thus records of her life) to be preserved in the dry desert sand until they were discovered in the last century. Even the powerful Thutmose, who became Egypt's greatest military leader, could not destroy the memory of the woman he detested!

Ancient Egypt's Greatest General

When Thutmose III took command of Egypt as pharaoh, he followed in the footsteps of his grandfather, Thutmose I. He quickly regained control of lands to the east that had drifted out of Egypt's grip during the reign of his stepmother, and he further expanded the empire all the way to the valley of the Tigris and Euphrates Rivers (in modern Iraq). His soldiers brought back stories about those strange rivers that seemed to flow backwards, for unlike the Nile that flowed from south to north, the Asian rivers flowed from north to south! The Egyptian army considered this natural phenomenon as peculiar as the customs of the local people. Thutmose was very interested in nature, and he found time to collect unusual plants and animals in the lands he visited; these were sent back to Egypt to be exhibited in a botanical garden at Thebes, the first of its kind. Thutmose also expanded his empire south all the way to the Fourth Cataract. Egypt now controlled a vast territory—it stretched one thousand miles from the Fourth Cataract to the Euphrates River.

Thutmose had a clever system to insure the loyalty of the eastern peoples he conquered: He required that the children of the ruling families be sent to live in the royal palace in Thebes, where they were raised with his own children. When the "visitors" came of age, they returned to their native soils, totally "Egyptianized" and loyal to the pharaoh. Thutmose also won the support of the native government officials by creating new positions for them within the structure of the Egyptian imperial state. He kept them under his control by depriving them of any financial power.

Thutmose demanded tribute payments from the nations of his eastern empire; the jewels, spices, and other luxurious trinkets sent to Thebes from the east combined with the gold mined in Nubia enabled the upper classes of Egyptian society to enjoy a level of luxury they had never known, even in the prosperous Middle Kingdom. Egypt was now the richest nation in the ancient world, the envy of all neighboring nations of the Mediterranean. A Greek writer remarked that in those times the gold in Egypt was as common as dust!

The pharaohs of the 18th Dynasty used a sizeable portion of their great wealth to build grandiose temples; the awe-inspiring temple at Karnak in Thebes was the largest one ever constructed. In fact, the New Kingdom was Egypt's golden age of art and architecture.

An End to Patriotism

The population of the Egyptian empire at this time was nine million people! The numbers of subjects as well as the expanse of territory had grown so dramatically that the pharaohs were forced to delegate an increasingly greater proportion of their power to the nobles. There was simply too much for one monarch to manage. As a result, the bureaucracy of government officials became very complex and unwieldy. We have already learned how this happened (on a smaller scale) at the end of the Old Kingdom.

The growth of the empire also affected the makeup of the army. Unlike earlier times when the troops were all inhabitants of the Nile Valley and, as such, totally loyal to the pharaoh, by the New Kingdom a large percentage of the army was made up of mercenaries (soldiers of foreign nationalities hired to fight for the pharaoh) whose main interest was getting paid. As a result, the patriotism felt among the ranks in earlier times was gone, and a monarch could no longer depend upon the unquestioning obedience of his fighting men.

A Different Kind of Monarch

In 1361 B.C.E., a young man named Amonhotep IV assumed the throne of Egypt. He was surely the nation's most eccentric monarch, but he had a great (although temporary) influence upon Egyptian religion, art and literature. We shall learn more about his accomplishments in Chapter 5. Unfortunately, his preoccupation with new ideas about religion and art prevented him from effectively governing the vast territory that he had inherited, and the Asian nations gradually regained their independence. The unquestioned authority that Thutmose III had held over his empire would never be known by another pharaoh. When Amonhotep died, his son-in-law, the boy Tutankhaten (later Tutankhamon) became pharaoh, and the priests and government officials immediately began to undo all of the late ruler's work. In a short time, the eccentric monarch was completely forgotten.

Ramses the Great

Toward the end of the New Kingdom there were eleven pharaohs named Ramses. Studied collectively, their period of history is known as the Rameside. The founder of the dynasty, Ramses I, reconquered much of the eastern empire that had been lost by Amonhotep. His son Ramses II, or Ramses the Great as he preferred to be known, is the most famous pharaoh of this period. He ruled for sixty-six years.

Like most of the pharaohs of the New Kingdom, Ramses II led his warriors into battle. His goal was to carry on his father's plans to regain all of the old empire. However, there is much question about his role in history. It seems that he was a bit of a braggart, and the descriptions of his military exploits that he ordered inscribed upon the walls of his temples and tomb were apparently great exaggerations. Such distortions of the truth are documented by accounts written at the time by eyewitnesses to these battles, accounts suggesting that any successes on the part of the Pharaoh were often a matter of luck! For example, Ramses was most proud of his "great victory" over the Hittites, a warrior race from the east. When the two armies met in Kadesh, Syria, the three-man chariots of the Hittites proved to be superior to the smaller Egyptian vehicles, and two of Ramses' top squadrons were easily routed. Some of the Pharaoh's men fled to his camp (not a good beginning for a major battle). At this point, Ramses' account states that he prayed to the god Amon for strength and then led his men back into battle, where they swiftly destroyed the enemy forces. The truth seems to be that after their initial victory the

Ramses the Great

pharaohs scratched off of obelisks (tall stone columns) and replaced with his own! He built temples honoring the god Amon and enlarged those that already stood, including the great temple at Karnak. He filled many of the sanctuaries with statues of himself! Ramses lived a long life—he outlived eleven of his sons and died peacefully in his eighties.

The temples, monuments and statues of Ramses the Great today lie in ruins. One of the broken statues inspired the nineteenth century English poet Percy Bysshe Shelley to write the following lines in his famous poem *Ozymandias*:

> I met a traveler from an antique land
> Who said: Two vast and trunkless legs of
> Stone
> Stand in the desert...Near them, on the
> sand,
> Half sunk, a shattered visage lies, whose
> frown,
> And wrinkled lip, and sneer of cold
> command,
> Tell that its sculptor well those passions
> read
> Which yet survive, stamped on these
> lifeless things,
> The hand that mocked them, and the
> heart that fed:
> And on the pedestal these words appear:
> "My name is Ozymandias, king of kings:
> Look on my works, ye Mighty, and
> despair!"
> Nothing beside remains. Round the decay
> Of that colossal wreck, boundless and bare
> The lone and level sands stretch far away.

Hittites let down their guard and prepared to loot Ramses' camp. They had to quickly reassemble when they saw the Egyptian army advancing toward them. The battle ended in a stalemate, with both sides considerably weakened by the experience.

But no matter how it happened, Ramses did manage to subdue the Hittites. In 1283 B.C.E. he signed a peace treaty with those warriors that recognized Egypt's control of Palestine and southern Syria. This was the world's first formal peace treaty. To strengthen his relations with his former enemies, he married a Hittite princess, although, his first wife, Nefertari, remained his favorite spouse.

Ramses' supreme egotism is reflected by the countless monuments he had built in his own honor up and down the banks of the Nile. In fact, he erected more buildings and colossal statues than any other Egyptian ruler. He ordered that these monuments be covered with hieroglyphs testifying to his greatness. He even had the names of former

For all his boasting, Ramses was only mortal.

The Emergence of Foreign Rulers

The expansion of the Egyptian empire during the New Kingdom gradually weakened the central authority of the pharaoh. Over the years, the bureaucrats subtly assumed more and more power, and by the 20th Dynasty the status of the pharaoh was seriously in question. When a sovereign was especially weak, the army generals often stepped in to restore order, and this put the military in a position of great power and influence. At the same time, even the priesthood was becoming very powerful. In the reign of Ramses III a vast migration of nomads from Greece, the Mediterranean islands and Asia Minor known as the Sea People, threatened Egypt. Ramses fought them off as best he could, but Egypt narrowly escaped being conquered. During this struggle the eastern empire was lost, never to be regained. The succeeding rulers were weak and ineffective (among them eight more kings named Ramses), and several factions of nobles and priests who vied with one another for absolute power controlled the government. At one point, a high priest named Herihor actually ruled Upper Egypt under the nominal authority of the pharaoh.

In the end, Egypt fell under the rule of Africans from Lybia and Nubia and then of Asians. The foreign monarchs provided stability for a while, but they could not prevent the invasion of Egypt by the invincible armies of the Persians, a warlike people from western Asia (modern Iran).

The Final Years

The Persians reigned for two hundred years until Alexander the Great of Macedonia conquered Egypt in 332 B.C.E. The Egyptian people welcomed the Greek military genius as a hero because he had delivered them from the hated Persians. Alexander respected the art and religion of the Egyptians, and he even trekked to a temple in an oasis in the western desert to honor one of their gods. He ordered a great city (Alexandria) to be built in the delta, although he never lived to see it.

When Alexander died, the Egyptian portion of his empire was seized by one of his generals, Ptolemy. This is how a Greek founded Egypt's last dynasty. Alexandria became the capital of Egypt and a great

Ramses II at Abu Simbel.

center of learning in the ancient world of the Mediterranean. The city had good harbors, guarded by a giant lighthouse that was considered one of the seven wonders of the ancient world. It also contained a theater, a vast library, and a center for scholarly research.

The last member of the Ptolemy Dynasty to rule was the famous Cleopatra (VII). She was a highly intelligent and well educated woman, who had great dreams for her kingdom, but unfortunately it became a jewel in the crown of the emperor of Rome. Cleopatra was the wife of Julius Caesar and later of Marc Antony. According to legend, she submitted to a fatal snakebite when it became clear that her power was gone.

As the Nile valley became a Roman province in 30 C.E., the rich civilization that had flourished there for so many centuries continued to fade. The Romans closed all temples (some were later converted into Christian churches) and they stripped numerous Egyptian monuments of materials for their own buildings.

After the fall of Rome in the fifth century C.E., Egypt was ruled by the Arabs, a Moslem people who stamped out what was left of the ancient culture. Egypt would not regain independence until the twentieth century.

Questions

1. What are the three major time periods of ancient Egypt?

2. How did Egypt's geography contribute to the development of a highly organized central government?

3. With what foreign nations did Egypt trade during the Old Kingdom? What products did these nations offer in trade?

4. What is cuneiform?

5. What was the major achievement in architecture associated with the Old Kingdom?

The lighthouse at Alexandria

6. What did the anarchy of the Dark Ages make clear to the rulers of the Middle Kingdom?

7. Why did Egypt conquer Nubia?

8. Describe the Hyksos.

9. What attitude characterized the pharaoh's of the New Kingdom?

10. Where did Hatshepsut focus her energy?

11. Why did Thutmose III dislike Hatshepsut?

12. Why has Thutmose III been called the Egyptian Napoleon?

13. How did Amonhotep IV differ from other Pharaohs?

14. Describe the personality of Ramses II.

15. Who delivered Egypt from the rule of the Persians?

Further Thoughts

1. Ramses II is most likely the pharaoh referred to in the Old Testament. According to the Bible story, Moses led the Hebrews to freedom across the Red Sea; the waters parted to let the Hebrews escape and then washed over and drowned the pursuing army of the Pharaoh. Many historians believe that the Red Sea referred to in the Bible was in reality the Reed Sea, a small river in the eastern part of the marshy delta. They claim that the charioteers of the pharaoh pursued the fleeing Hebrews because the local officials did not wish to lose so many skilled laborers. They had to give up the chase when their horses and chariots got bogged down in the mire of the swamp!

2. We have seen that the Egyptians were by nature suspicious of foreigners. Although they were willing to trade with other

societies, they tended to view outsiders as socially and culturally inferior to themselves.

The building of Alexandria placed the Egyptians in the uncomfortable position of being second class citizens in their own country. The Greeks governed Egypt for several hundred years, and although they were respectful of Egypt's rich culture, they imposed their own ideas of science, religion and art upon the land they had conquered. Alexandria became a conclave of Greek scientists and learned men, and Greek was the official language of the entire nation. This occupation by the Greeks must have been as humiliating for the Egyptians as was their domination by the Hyksos at the end of the Middle Kingdom.

On the positive side, the Greeks did record many of the scientific discoveries of the Egyptians in their own language, and in this way they preserved much of ancient Egypt's cultural heritage.

3. An anthropologist named Thor Heyerdahl believed that the ancient Egyptians had once sailed in papyrus boats across the Atlantic Ocean to the New World. He based his theory on the fact that early North American Indians (the Maya, the Aztecs and the Mound Builders) designed pyramid-shaped structures. Other supporting evidence was the written language of the Micmac Indians, whose symbols vaguely resembled Egyptian hieroglyphs. In 1969 Heyerdahl built a boat from papyrus reeds copying those depicted upon the walls of ancient Egyptian tombs, and with a crew he sailed it across the Atlantic. The boat was named the Ra, after the Egyptian god of the sun. He had almost reached the coast of South America when the boat broke apart during a storm in the Caribbean Sea.

Undaunted, Heyerdahl built another boat (the Ra II), and this time he made it! He believed that his voyage proved that the Egyptians visited the New World thousands of years ago.

Many scientists agreed with his theory. When some preserved potatoes were found in an Egyptian tomb (potatoes were native to the New World), Heyerdahl's view seemed to be proven true. How could these vegetables have gotten to Egypt if they had not been brought back from the New World on Egyptian boats?

Other scientists discount Heyrdahl's theory, stating that the Egyptians were not the least bit adventurous, preferring the security of the Nile Valley. They suggest that if any ancient sailors made it to the New World, they were the Phoenicians, a people living in modern Lebanon who loved the sea.

4. The Egyptians had a grisly way of counting the number of enemy dead after a battle. They cut off the right hands of the enemy corpses, placed them in piles, and then counted the hands in each pile!

Projects

1. Draw a series of maps to illustrate the growth of the Egyptian nation. In the first one, show Egypt during the Old Kingdom (include the Sinai peninsula). In the second, show Egypt of the Middle Kingdom (include Nubia to the Third Cataract, and the Fayum). In the third map show the Egyptian empire at its greatest expanse. Consult books in your classroom or library, or check out the Internet.

2. Thutmose III has been called the Napoleon of ancient Egypt. Although he was only five feet four inches tall, he was

Egypt's mightiest warrior! Find out who the original Napoleon was, and write a short paper comparing his military goals and accomplishments with those of Thutmose.

3.   Queen Nefertiti, wife of Amonhotep IV (later called Akhenaten) is considered the most beautiful woman of ancient Egypt. In fact, her name means "the beautiful one is come." Learn more about her and write a short report.

4.   Learn more about Ramses III and "the Sea People." Write a short report about the naval battles he fought against them.

5.   Cleopatra was romantically involved with two great Roman generals. Find out who they were and write a short report.

6.   Research the history of the bow and arrow in ancient Egypt. Check out the advantages of the composite bow over the simple bow of earlier times. Write a short report. Be sure to include illustrations showing the design of different types of bows.

7.   Make a chart detailing the major events of each of the three main periods of ancient Egyptian history.

CHAPTER 4

WRITING

The concept of drawing symbols to record the words of a spoken language came to Egypt via traders and settlers from Asia. As we have seen, the Sumerians of Mesopotamia (the land between the Tigris and Euphrates Rivers in modern Iraq) were the first to experiment with writing. They used reeds gathered at the river's edge to make wedge-shaped marks on wet mud-bricks. Once the bricks dried in the hot sun, they became extremely permanent records. Thousands of such tablets exist to this day. The Sumerian writing is called *cuneiform* (meaning "wedge-shaped"), and its original purpose was to record business transactions.

Early Experiments With Writing

Around the time of Menes, cuneiform tablets had found their way to the Nile Valley. The Egyptians studied the tablets and experimented with new forms of writing, drawing pictures on bricks made from the Nile's mud to represent specific objects. For example, a drawing of a bull beside a stick figure of a man meant that someone owned the bull, a circle with a dot in the center stood for the sun, and a wavy line indicated water. Such symbols are called pictographs (picture writing). Some symbols had more than one meaning. For example, the half circle meant hill, but it also meant foreign,

since the Nile Valley is very flat and anything hilly was definitely alien to the local environment.

Many objects could be easily drawn as pictographs, but abstract ideas such as love and happiness were more difficult to represent. At first, the Egyptians dealt with this predicament by drawing picture puzzles (rebuses) in which the names of particular objects, when pronounced together, sounded like something else. An example of a rebus in English is a picture of a bee placed beside one of a leaf to represent the word "belief." But this system had its limitations, and so the Egyptians began to use pictures to represent specific sounds. Over the years, certain symbols became the standard "letters" for particular sounds. Some symbols stood for compound sounds such as th or ch.

Symbols that Reflect the Natural World

The Egyptians selected their writing symbols from the natural environment. Their "letters" include pictures of owls, quail chicks, water, parts of the human body (such as hands, arms, and feet), vultures, reeds, knotted ropes, loaves of bread, and feathers. When a symbol had more than one meaning, they drew a mark called a determinative to indicate which meaning was intended. For example, a pair of walking legs next to a particular symbol indicated that the word was an action verb.

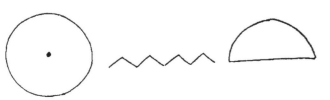

Pictographs

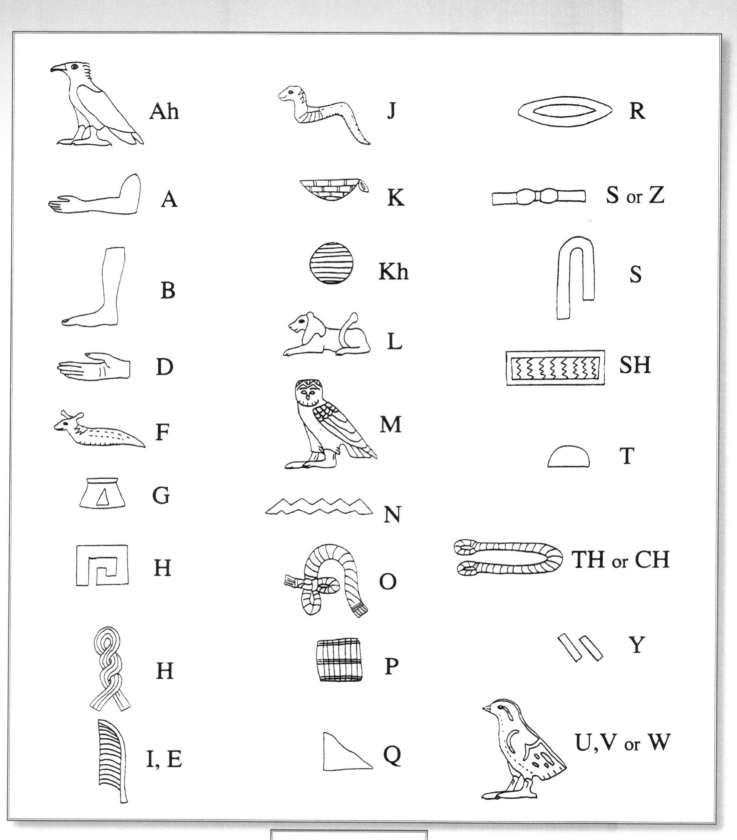

An alphabet of hieroglyphs

The Number of Signs and Symbols Grows

Over the years, the Egyptian written language evolved into a combination of pictographs, symbols representing sounds, and determinatives. New symbols were frequently added, but the conservative Egyptians didn't eliminate any of the old ones. During the New Kingdom there were over seven hundred in everyday use!

Some key sound symbols were employed frequently, and they could be used alone in a sort of shorthand to describe many simple ideas. Unfortunately, this is the closest that the Egyptians ever came to developing an alphabet. Their reluctance to eliminate any of the word pictures that had been used by generations of writers prevented them from making the breakthrough in communication that a simple alphabet would have brought. Instead, they continued to expand their cumbersome collection of signs and symbols, leaving it to another Mediterranean people, the Phoenicians, to create the world's first true alphabet.

Where the Hieroglyphs Were Written

The Greek word *hieroglyph* means "sacred carved writing." Egyptian picture writing is called hieroglyphic because it was often carved (and painted) on the walls of tombs and temples. But the symbols were also carved on state monuments, and they were painted on the sides of wooden coffins as well as upon Egyptian paper (papyrus). Many scholars feel that it is the most beautiful writing ever designed. The Egyptians called their written language *medu netcher* ("the words of the gods").

How To Read Hieroglyphs

Hieroglyphs can be read from right to left or from left to right. The determining factor is the direction in which the pictures of people and animals face: if they face left, the message is read from left to right, and if they face right, the opposite is true. (In other words, always read toward the face of the animal!). Hieroglyphs can also be read in columns proceeding from top to bottom (see below). There is no punctuation, but the

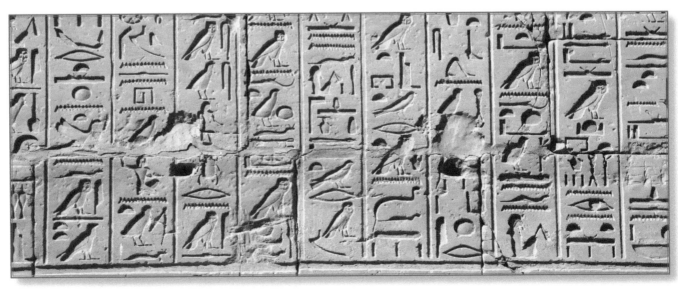

beginning of a new sentence is often painted in a different color.

The Egyptians were very frugal people, and this is reflected in the way that their writing utilized every bit of available space. If two small symbols were part of a single word, the writer simply drew one above the other in the space of a single average-sized "letter." And, not surprisingly, there were no spaces between words.

As we learned earlier, the symbols representing the name of a pharaoh were enclosed in an oval of braided rope that the French called a *cartouche* (their word for an oval-shaped bullet shell). These cartouches appear in great number on the walls of the royal tombs and other monuments from the Old Kingdom onward. The rope was meant to set the divine ruler apart from more worldly objects.

Other Forms of Writing

Great skill, time and patience were required for the painting and carving of hieroglyphs. Ordinary matters such as business transactions, letters, and stories were written in a script (cursive) version of hieroglyphs called hieratic. It was read from right to left, as is modern Hebrew. In the eighth century B.C.E., the Egyptians created demotic, an even more rapidly written shorthand used for legal documents.

The Scribes

Most writing was produced by a small elite group of men known as the scribes. They made up a large part of the two percent of Egyptian society that could read and write (the remaining literate people were the priests, nobles, and royalty). The scribes enjoyed great power and job security, since the government always needed someone to record its transactions. And they never had to pay any taxes! Talented scribes could develop other talents and become architects or important government officials such as tax collectors. A scribe named Horemheb even became pharaoh!

The education of a scribe began at a young age. Nine-year-old boys from noble families were eligible to attend schools in the temples where the priests taught reading, writing and mathematics. Occasionally, the son of a peasant who seemed exceptionally gifted was given a chance to study with the more privileged boys. The sons of scribes learned their craft directly from their fathers. School hours were long and much of the work was rather boring. The boys sat on hard stones practicing hundreds of hieroglyphic symbols over and over again. The teachers were strict, and they abided by the popular saying of the time, "a boy's ears were on his backside." In other words, the more he was beaten the better he would listen! It took many years to master hieroglyphs and hieratic, but once he completed his education, a young scribe could look forward to a comfortable life.

Papyrus plants growing along the banks of the Nile

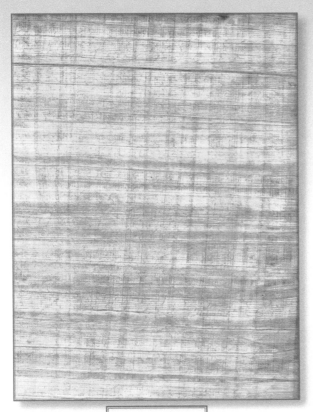

Sheet of papyrus

The World's First Paper

The Egyptians were the first people to write on paper. It was made from the papyrus plant that grew abundantly in the Nile delta. The paper was much less fragile than clay tablets (it couldn't be broken) and more easily transported (it was light).

Preparing sheets of papyrus was a simple process. Once the papyrus reeds were cut, the outer covering was removed, leaving the soft inner pith. This was cut into thin strips. The strips were then laid crosswise in alternating layers (right to left and then up and down) upon a large stone. When the desired thickness was reached, a cloth was placed on top of the strips and the surface was pounded with a wooden mallet until the layers were compressed into a thin sheet. Then the cloth was removed and the papyrus was placed in the hot sun to dry. Finally, the dried sheet of papyrus was polished smooth with a

rough stone. Often several sheets were glued together with flour paste to form a scroll that could be rolled up. The Romans called the scrolls "volumen", and they were the world's first books. Our word *volume* dates back to these ancient scrolls.

Pen and Ink

A scribe wrote upon the papyrus with a rush pen (also made from the papyrus reed). He chewed on the end of the rush until the fibers were broken and could be shaped into a point. His palette was made from a rectangular piece of wood that had a slot to hold his pen and indentations that were scooped out for the ink. Ordinary black ink was made from soot, ground plants and water, while red ink was made from the red mineral ocre. The rainbow of colors used to decorate tombs came from a variety of ground-up minerals. The scribe traditionally sat cross-legged to write. His tightened kilt made a convenient "desk" upon which he placed his sheet of papyrus, while his palette of ink lay by his side.

A scribe

The Rosetta Stone.

The Discovery of the Rosetta Stone

When the civilization of ancient Egypt finally crumbled, hieroglyphs fell into disuse, and before long no one was able to decipher them. The meaning of the signs and symbols that so vividly described the lives of the early Nile dwellers remained a mystery for centuries. This changed in 1799, when the army of the French emperor Napoleon was in Egypt. One of the soldiers discovered a four-foot long black basalt stone protruding from the mud near the Rosetta Branch of the delta. Known as the Rosetta Stone, it bore a message that was chiseled in three kinds of writing: Greek, hieroglyphic and demotic.

The stone had been carved in 196 B.C.E., and it commemorated the coronation in Memphis of Ptolemy V (a pharaoh of Greek ancestry). Since it was easy to read the Greek, scholars at the time hoped that the stone would offer the key to the writing of ancient Egypt. But it was no easy task to decipher the writing, and it took a French scholar named Jean François Champollion twenty-two years to do it! The break-through came when he saw a connection between the "p" "e" and "o" in Cleopatra's name and these letters in Ptolemy's cartouche. Once the code was broken, scholars could begin to translate the writings of the tombs, temples, monuments, and volumes of papyrus. Archaeologists flocked to Egypt to unlock the secrets that had remained hidden for so long.

Questions

1. What ancient people was the first to write?
2. What are pictographs?
3. Describe five early Egyptian "letters."
4. What does the word "hieroglyph" mean?
5. What is a cartouche?
6. How are hieroglyphs read?
7. Why did the scribes have such comfortable lives?
8. How did the Egyptians make their paper?
9. Describe the pen and ink used by a scribe.
10. What is the Rosetta Stone?

Ideas to Think About

1. A few Egyptian words have found their way into modern English. The word "oasis" comes directly from Egyptian hieroglyphs, and "chemistry" derives from *kemi*.

2. The Egyptian language evolved very slowly, but it can be divided into several sub-groups: the tongues of the Old, Middle and New Kingdoms, Demotic (from 700 B.C.E. until 500 C.E.), and Coptic (from the third century through the Middle Ages). Since medieval times, the official language of Egypt has been Arabic.

3. Over the years, Egyptologists have collected thousands of pieces of papyrus bearing ancient Egyptian writing. As with the writing on the walls of tombs, temples and public monuments, they provide many clues about life in ancient Egypt. Archaeologists owe a great deal to Napoleon I of France. When that ambitious emperor led an expedition of 25,000 soldiers into Egypt, he also brought along 167 scientists and artists to study the ancient ruins. They eventually produced a twenty-four volume work (*The Description of Egypt*), which stirred a European interest in the ancient world. Egyptology, the

formal study of the civilization of ancient Egypt, dates from Napoleon's expedition.

Projects

1. Using old magazines, cut out a collection of colored pictures. Make a key, and then use the pictures to write a message in the style of Egyptian hieroglyphs. You can use these materials to play a game. Divide the class into two teams. Each team sends a message (made from cut out or drawn pictures) to the other. The messages are delivered at the same time. The team that deciphers its message first is the winner.

2. Study the chart on page 42 showing some common hieroglyphs. Then use the symbols to write the following message about yourself: My name is (your name) of (the name of your town), the (adjective describing yourself) and (another descriptive adjective). Consult books in your classroom to determine the proper colors of the "letters."

CHAPTER 5

RELIGION

[handwritten: write 3 characteristics of religous beliefs. write a quote after each characteristic]

[handwritten: maybe board of religion]

From earliest times the Egyptians were in awe of the creatures of the fertile valley—the beasts that grazed along the floodplain, the serpents that slithered across the mud, the birds that soared effortlessly in the cloudless sky, and the animals that swam in the cool waters of the Nile. They believed that immortal spirits inhabited the bodies of these creatures. As hunters, they knew their survival depended upon finding plenty of game, and so they worshipped the spirit of the species of beast they stalked. They hoped that by pleasing the spirit with their prayers and dances they could convince it to provide them with plenty of animals for their hunt. They also worshipped the spirits of dangerous animals like snakes and crocodiles, hoping that such reverence would prevent those creatures from doing them harm. Sobek, a crocodile god, became an important deity in many parts of Egypt. Other animals were considered sacred because of their usefulness. For example, the mongoose was revered because it devoured snakes. Cats were valued because they consumed pesky rodents, while dogs and geese warned of approaching strangers.

Every small village had its own special deities. The people of Naquada in Upper Egypt worshipped Seth, a fierce, long-snouted beast who seems a combination of wild dog and donkey. In nearby Nekhen, the people prayed to a strong and cunning falcon god known as Horus. Hawks and falcons were admired throughout Egypt not only for their swiftness but also for the way they hid from their prey by hovering between it and the sun; when the time was right, they attacked

A soaring falcon

with a burst of power, appearing to descend directly from the sun itself. As we shall see, Horus later became a major god of all of Egypt. Other deities included a ram called Khnum (according to some myths he created the first man), an ibis called Thoth (the god of writing and wisdom), and a cow called Hathor (the goddess of love and nurturing). Eventually, myths about the deities were combined with legends about local heroes; the result was a sort of biblical history of the land of the Nile.

Scholars have always wondered why Egyptian gods are often shown with the head of an animal but the body of a human being. The most likely explanation for such strange looking deities is that the priests wore masks of the animal gods to whom they were appealing when they performed religious ceremonies. Paintings were made of the masked priests, and these images became identified with the gods themselves. For this reason, Anubis is represented both as a sleek jackal and as a jackal-headed man, and Horus

Anubis depicted in two ways

has been painted and sculpted both as a falcon and a falcon-headed man.

The Story of Creation

The Egyptians did not understand the forces of nature, and so they invented stories to explain such natural events as the rising of the sun, the flooding of the Nile, and death itself.

The Egyptian version of the creation of the world began with a period known as Chaos when there was only water (called Nun). Slowly humps of land resembling tortoise shells appeared, just as they do after the flood waters of the Inundation recede. Upon one of these humps of land appeared the sun god Ra. He looked around and then created air and rivers. Geb later became the god of the earth and Nut the sky goddess. According to one telling of the story, humans (Egyptians, of course!) were made from the tears of Ra. In another version he spat them out!

The Power of the Sun

It is not surprising that the sun god was always the most important deity in Egypt. Imagine yourself in a desert: You are surrounded by dull-colored sand, rocks and pebbles that stretch endlessly to the horizon while overhead the intense heat of the sun mercilessly bakes your skin. That radiant sphere in the heavens is as much a force of death and destruction in the desert as it is one of life and abundance in more lush surroundings.

The ancient Egyptians were dazzled by the power of the sun, and the path it seemed to take across the sky every day fascinated them. To explain the daily movement of the sun, they imagined that each morning Ra launched his royal boat at the eastern horizon and then spent the daylight hours sailing across the sky. It was logical that the god should travel by boat, since that was the major means of transportation in the Nile Valley. He had to be on the constant lookout out for Apophis, an evil snake that always tried to swallow him. When this happened, there was an eclipse, which lasted until the snake spat him out again! At dusk Ra disappeared beyond the western horizon and traveled to the Land of the Dead, which lay beneath the earth (the Egyptians believed the world was flat). He sailed through that dark kingdom all night until he reached the eastern horizon, just at the break of dawn. Then he began his journey across the heavens and the cycle was repeated.

Such fanciful explanations of natural events comforted the early Egyptians. The story of Ra's journey explained the apparent movement of the sun, and so they ceased to

The sun god Ra

The Cycle Is Seen Everywhere

The daily pattern of light and darkness came to symbolize life, death and rebirth (didn't the sun always return?), and similar patterns were observed in other parts of the natural environment. One example was the annual cycle of the crops that thrived on the floodplain of the Nile. Seeds sown in the moist soil grew quickly into robust plants, but once the abundant wheat and barley grain was harvested, the plants withered and died. Just as the sun arose from the east and filled the sky with brightness and warmth, only to disappear beyond the western horizon at dusk, the plants sprang up from the soil, burst into flower and fruit, and then fell into decay. But like the morning sun ushered in a new day, new seeds newly planted took root and grew in the fields where the earlier crop had withered. The Egyptians associated the miracle of the annual harvest with a goddess called Isis.

The cycle of life, death and rebirth could even be seen in the flooding of the Nile. The farmers noticed that the Inundation always occurred at a time of the year when the sun reached a particular position among the stars. This observation fit in well with their belief that the sun god controlled every aspect of nature, including the rising of the waters of the Nile. They soon learned that by studying the configuration of stars in the heavens they could predict when the next Inundation would occur. (More about this later.) That enabled them to prepare for the flood waters by gathering in the last of their harvested crops and removing every useful possession from the floodplain. Once the Egyptian farmers understood the cycle of the river, they no longer worried when they saw

worry about whether there would be light again after the darkness of night.

The ancient Egyptians envisioned Ra as a man with the head of a falcon on top of which rested the disc of the sun. So his image embodied two very important symbols of desert life.

its waters rising. They knew that their fields would be flooded for only a few months, and that once the waters did recede the land would have been fertilized with a new layer of silt. They associated the river that brought life to their strip of land with a god named Hapi. Just as the sun god Ra provided the beneficial light and warmth of the sun, Hapi produced the water and rich soil so necessary to the farmers' crops. According to one myth, Hapi released the waters from a bottomless jar as he sat in a cavern below the mountains of Aswan, protected by magic serpents. An ancient song to the river begins: "Hail to you, O Nile, who flows from the earth and comes to keep Egypt alive."

Belief in an Afterlife

All around them, then, the early Egyptians observed a pattern of life, death and rebirth, and they began to wonder if this miraculous cycle might apply to their own

Ra in his boat

lives as well. People were born, they grew up and worked very hard producing food for themselves and their families, they became old, and then they died. Was it possible that, like the sun and the crops, they too could return to life again? Belief in an afterlife would surely remove their fears of death.

They expressed their hopes for their own rebirth in an allegorical version of the daily voyage of Ra: The sun god began his journey in the eastern skies as a child, reached the zenith of the heavens at noon as a young man, and arrived at the western horizon as an old man. He then died and spent the night in the Land of the Dead, only to be miraculously reborn the next morning, ready to begin his heavenly journey all over again.

The belief that there might be another life after this one led the Nile dwellers to bury the bodies of their dead in shallow pits in the desert sand along with tools, cooking implements and even food. They hoped that once the sand and pebbles covered the deceased person he would begin another life. That is why he needed the tools and food. When viewed in this way, death was not an end but a new beginning.

The Myth of Osiris

This preoccupation with death led to the creation of a series of myths designed to explain the miracle of rebirth. The central figure was a god named Osiris, the god of the dead. According to the stories, Osiris had once been the king of Egypt, ruling fairly and benevolently with his wife Isis (she would later become the goddess of the harvest). He taught his people about art and agriculture.

Osiris had a wicked brother named Seth (the same fellow who was the god

Anubis.

this would permanently rid him of Osiris so that he could become king!

Once again the devoted Isis searched along the banks of the river, where she gathered each of the fourteen pieces of her husband. She took these to Anubis, a god personified by a jackal. Anubis wrapped the fourteen pieces together with strips of linen and restored Osiris to life. This miracle explains why Anubis became the god of mummies. (The jackal is like a wild dog that lives in the desert. Since jackals were common in the western sands where Ra disappeared beyond the horizon every evening, they were also associated with the Land of the Dead. For this reason, Anubis

of Naquada) who wanted to be king. One evening Seth invited Osiris and Isis along with several other guests to dinner. After the meal, he produced a beautiful chest and said that he would give it to the person who could most comfortably fit inside it. When Osiris climbed into the chest, the evil Seth slammed down the lid! Then he threw it into the Nile where it quickly drifted downstream with the current. Isis and her sister Nephthys patiently searched for the chest. They finally discovered it tangled among the roots of a tree in modern day Lebanon. They rescued Osiris and brought him back to Egypt. But again Seth entered the scene. He slew his brother and cut his body into fourteen pieces, which he threw into the Nile. Surely,

Tomb painting of Osiris and Isis

Wall carving of Horus

was also considered the protector of the dead.)

Osiris and Isis had a son, Horus (the god of Nekhen, personified by a falcon). After his son's birth, Osiris went to the Underworld and became the god of the dead. The Egyptians also considered Osiris the god of vegetation and fertility, believing that he brought the farmers' fields back to life just as Anubis had restored his own existence. He is always depicted in paintings as a bound mummy with a gruesome greenish face (green being the color of vegetation).

Horus grew to manhood. He was determined to avenge his father's death, so he challenged his wicked uncle Seth to a fight. Seth cut out Horus's eye, but it was later magically restored by the god Thoth (the eye of Horus became a symbol for good

or restored health). Horus defeated his uncle and became the king of Egypt. Seth was banished from the fertile valley of the Nile and forced to live eternally in the barren wasteland of the desert. He became the god of violence (the Egyptians considered the desert a very hostile place). The sandstorms that occasionally blew in from the western sands and destroyed the crops were blamed on Seth. The Egyptians worshipped Seth in order to appease him and to prevent him from inflicting his evil upon them.

The pharaohs of the Middle Kingdom identified themselves with Osiris and his son. In fact, the reigning pharaoh was believed to incarnate (represent) Horus. Upon his death, the king's soul became one with Osiris in the Land of the Dead. The new pharaoh then became the living Horus. At the funeral of a pharaoh, the priests would chant, "The Hawk has flown to the heavens, and another stands in his place."

The Power of Ma'at

As a living god as well as chief priest of Egypt, the pharaoh was in charge of maintaining order and righteousness throughout the kingdom. The Egyptians referred to the state of perfect harmony as Ma'at; it was personified by a goddess of the same name who was often depicted with outstretched wings. She wore an ostrich feather, which became the symbol of balance and harmony. Remember how the Egyptians believed that Egypt arose as a hump or mound of land out of the waters of Chaos? According to their myths, the Egyptian society had flourished since the original Chaos because of its ability to maintain order. When Ma'at was upheld

The winged goddess Ma'at (left) and the goddess Hathor.

Egypt prospered, the Nile flooded its banks to an appropriate level, the fields produced an abundance of crops, and all enemies were kept at bay. When Ma'at was disturbed, there was a return to Chaos. The concept of Ma'at clearly reflects the love of order and stability that pervaded Egyptian culture and it helps to explain that ancient people's utter disdain for anything that might upset the everyday pattern and rhythm of life in the Nile Valley.

So Many Deities

Over the centuries, the myths about the gods and goddesses became more and more complex as new deities were added to the list. Being a conservative people, the Egyptians never considered eliminating any old beliefs when new ones were acquired. And so by the end of the New Kingdom their religion had become a complicated network of relationships among over two thousand deities! Some gods, such as Osiris and Ra, were worshipped by all Egyptians, while many local gods were only worshipped by the inhabitants of a small area. Gods of special interest to ordinary people up and down the Nile included Taweret, the goddess of childbirth, Bes, the god of pleasure, and the cobra goddess Meretseger (she was worshipped to prevent the possibility of snakebites!).

You've probably noticed that the gods and goddesses pictured in this book carry an object in one hand. It looks like a cross with a loop at the top. This is an ankh - the Egyptian symbol for eternal life.

Ancient statue of a cat

Sacred Animals

The many animals that the Egyptians considered sacred led very comfortable lives. For example, the cats that protected the grain from rodents were greatly pampered. When they died, the family members shaved their eyebrows as a sign of mourning. A dead cat's body was mummified and given a special funeral. The spirit of the cat (symbolized by the goddess Bastet) was called "miu"—this certainly suggests that cats around the world have always made the same sound!

Bulls were sacred to Ptah, the god of craftsmen in the city of Memphis. A special bull referred to as Apis lived on the grounds of Ptah's temple. The Egyptians believed that the spirit of the god entered the bull during religious ceremonies. His dung was used for magical and medicinal purposes! Apis was black with a white triangular patch between his horns. He also had a patch resembling a flying vulture on his back, a scarab-shaped lump on his tongue, and double hairs in his tail. When he died, a search was made all over Egypt to locate his successor. It must

have been extremely difficult to find a bull that met all the physical requirements! The dead bull was mummified and buried, adorned with golden jewelry, in a huge granite coffin. The Serapeum is an enormous underground tomb in Saqqara (the funerary district west of Memphis). It contains the mummified remains of sixty-four Apis bulls that were buried over the span of one thousand years.

Even monkeys were revered. Because the baboons made such a commotion at sunrise, the Egyptians thought that they were worshipping Ra. This is why baboons became sacred creatures.

In 10 B.C.E. the priests at Lake Moeris (in the Fayum) had a sacred crocodile that they tamed and fed with cakes and honey wine! Archaeologists have discovered a pit near the river valley containing hundreds of mummified crocodiles. These were sacred animals, and the ancient Egyptians made sure that they were properly buried. To give the bodies shape, the embalmers stuffed the inner cavities with old rolls of papyrus, much as we use newspaper as filler when

Carved image of Apis

we mail packages. The papyrus contained information about such ordinary aspects of life as the price of duck and the amount of grain harvested in a particular field. These mundane facts and figures recovered from the wrinkled-up papyrus are for us priceless records of a civilization long gone.

The ancient Egyptians often drew pictures of the scarab beetle on the walls of their tombs and they placed small amulets of this creature with their mummies. This insect lays its eggs in a small pile of animal dung, which it tirelessly pushes around until the eggs hatch. The sight of the baby beetles emerging from a pile of dirt seemed miraculous to the ancient Egyptians, and it reminded them of the tender young plants that burst through the rich soil of the Nile valley soon after they were planted. For this reason, the scarab beetle became a symbol of regeneration and rebirth. Placing a scarab beetle in a tomb was intended to help the deceased person achieve an afterlife.

The Temples

Egyptian temples were like palaces for the gods. They were built in every city, and each one had the same basic design of courtyards and walkways leading to a central sanctuary, where a golden statue of the god was kept in a shrine. Although the spirit of a god was believed to move about freely, it sought repose within the statue made in its image. Only priests were allowed into the sanctuary, for only they had the power to communicate with the gods and to interpret the divine messages for the people. The traditional posture of prayer was arms spread outward. This symbolized the belief that the god's power extended beyond the body (statue) it inhabited.

The villages of Egypt had small shrines that the ordinary people could enter, and many houses contained small statues of gods and goddesses for family worship.

The Priesthood

The office of the priesthood was handed down from father to son. High priests spent their entire lives at the temples. Other lesser priests were in fact nobles who performed their religious duties one month out of every four. The priests followed very strict rules of cleanliness, bathing in a pool of sacred water four times a day to purify themselves and shaving their bodies two times a day. They removed all body hair including eyebrows and lashes. They dressed in white linen robes (and occasionally in panther skins). As we have learned, the pharaoh was the high priest of all of Egypt. He conducted the important religious ceremonies dealing with the annual flood and the fertility of the soil.

Each morning the temple priests would "awaken" the god dwelling in the sanctuary, singing his praises. The high priest slowly approached the golden statue chanting, "I am the Pure One," and burning incense.

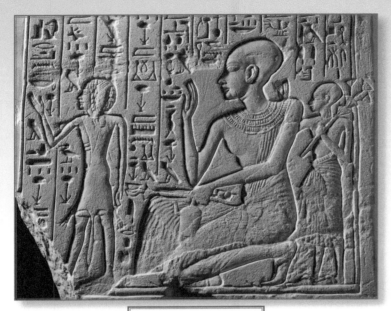

Carving of a high priest

He draped a fresh linen robe on the statue (removing the one from the night before) and then offered the god food that had been collected from the local farmers—bread, figs and grapes, perhaps a roast duck, and, of course, a vessel of wine. Later, the priests would eat the food, sharing its "essence" with the god. The statue received three meals a day, and at night it was covered with a fresh robe so that it could rest comfortably! The priests always swept the floor in front of them as they backed out of the sanctuary in order to erase their footprints and hence all trace of human presence.

Women could be priestesses, and many of them became quite powerful. The priestesses of Amon were considered the brides of the god. The priestesses added rhythm to ritual music by shaking sacred rattles called sistra or flailing their beaded necklaces.

Apart from religious duties, the priests passed on their knowledge of reading and writing to the next generation of learned men. This was their greatest legacy. They also kept accurate accounts of the grain and produce paid in taxes by the local farmers and stored in the temple warehouses. Some

of the temples owned large amounts of land, which brought in a great deal of income. Managing these funds gave the priests a lot of clout in the Egyptian economy.

Traveling Deity

Temples were the domain of the gods and the priests. Ordinary people were not allowed in even the temple courtyards because they were considered impure. (Remember how often the priests bathed to make themselves pure.) And, as we've learned, only the priests could communicate with the gods. The people's opportunity to see a divine figure came on special occasions when the statue of an important deity was carried from its temple in a ceremonial boat that rested upon the shoulders of the priests. It might journey to the center of the city where all the local inhabitants could view it, or it might be placed on a larger boat on the river and taken to another city to "visit" the statue of another god. The farmers would pause from their work in the fields as the boat passed by. What a magical moment it must have been for them.

Although it does seem strange to treat a statue in such a way, we must remember that magic played a major role in ancient times, and the Egyptians did not question a god's ability to inhabit an object, be it a golden statue or the body of an animal. The Egyptians often wore amulets (small statues of the gods) for good luck. They used magic wands of ivory (shaped like boomerangs) to draw circles around their sleeping quarters to prevent being stung by scorpions or bitten by snakes. A picture of Horus with a handful of snakes and scorpions was often painted on the wall of a house to keep those nasty creatures away.

Egypt's Great Religious Experiment

The religion that evolved during the Old Kingdom changed very little in its basic beliefs during the three thousand years of ancient Egyptian civilization. Only once was there a break with the deeply rooted traditions, and this was but a brief interlude.

In 1361 B.C.E., a young man named Amonhotep IV became the pharaoh. As a child, Amonhotep had learned from his mother about a cult that worshipped the sun exclusively, and he was drawn to this new religion that differed so radically from the Egyptian worship of countless gods and goddesses. When he became pharaoh, he used his power to revolutionize the state religion, and his subjects were suddenly jolted out of their familiar patterns of worship. Amonhotep boldly proclaimed that there was only one god, known as Aten, who was the creative force of the universe. Paintings and relief pictures chiseled into stone during this period depict Aten as a

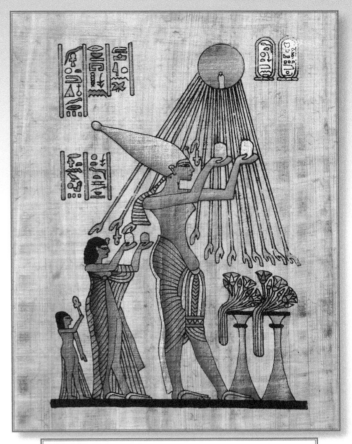

Akhenaten and Nefertiti make an offering to Aten

large circular sun disc from which extend rays of light. At the ends of some of the rays are outstretched hands holding the symbol for life (the ankh). This image was certainly a change from such semi-human deities as Anubis and Isis.

Amonhotep banned the worship of all the traditional Egyptian gods who had played so great a role in the lives of the Nile dwellers for tens of centuries. All temples were closed. Priests, who up until then had enjoyed a comfortable and lofty status, suddenly found themselves out of work, unless they were willing to renounce their old religion and convert to the worship of Aten.

Amonhotep even changed his name to Akhenaten, which means "pleasing to Aten." He realized that it would be awkward to convert the old temples into holy shrines

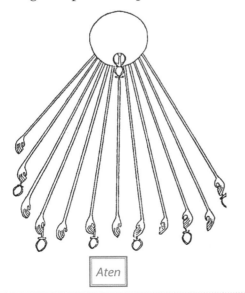

Aten

for Aten, so he ordered the construction of an entire new city, Akhetaten (meaning "the city of the horizon of Aten") 250 miles downstream from Thebes. Akhetaten became the new capital of Egypt as well as the site of a magnificent temple dedicated to Aten. It was an open air temple so that the worshippers could directly experience the warm presence of the sun.

Akhenaten's revolutionary ideas affected art and literature as well as religion. The Pharaoh personally wrote many beautiful hymns to Aten that have survived to this day. Because the new religion was supposed to "live on truth," he ordered that all art must reflect truth and reality. Artists were encouraged to be creative and innovative. Paintings from the period show they explored the play of light and shadow and attempted to suggest different perspectives of depth. They even combined different materials to create new textures. Rejecting the stiff, formal style in which artists had always portrayed the royal family, Akenaten encouraged a new, more natural presentation. While earlier monarchs had been immortalized in regal poses, he allowed himself to be painted in informal settings with his beautiful wife Nefertiti and their three small daughters. This more realistic portrayal of the royal family gives us a good idea of what Akhenaten looked like. He might have suffered from a glandular disorder, because he appears to have a distorted, thin face with very full lips and very little chin, a narrow chest, wide hips and a large pot belly. His looks clearly did not inspire great reverence, and they must have deeply offended the Egyptian people who enjoyed thinking of their monarchs as unapproachable gods! It seems a strange

Akhenaten

irony that this grotesque monarch was married to the woman generally considered the most beautiful of all Egyptians. Or perhaps the new style encouraged the artists to exaggerate minor physical abnormalities. We will never know for certain how the pharaoh appeared.

Akhenaten's new religion was not generally well received, but most government officials and many priests grudgingly moved to the new capital city and at least pretended to worship Aten. Yet, as we have learned, the Egyptians were reluctant to change their ways, and archaeologists have found many statues of the traditional gods among the ruins of Akhenaten's new capital. Apparently those who embraced the new religion did so only halfheartedly, and they continued to worship the old gods in the confines of their own homes.

When Akhenaten died, his son-in-law Tutankhaten (a young boy) became pharaoh. Immediately, the priests and government officials rushed to remove all the changes Akhenaten had made and to bring back the good old days. The boy's name was changed to Tutankhamon (replacing the name of Aten with that of Amon, the sun god of Thebes). Akhetaten was abandoned and Thebes was once again the capital. The revolutionary ideas of Akhenaten were quickly and completely forgotten.

Today, most countries of the world have a monotheistic religion (the worship of a single god). Egypt itself is inhabited mostly by Muslims, who worship a god called Allah. Perhaps Akhenaten was simply too far ahead of his time.

Questions

1. How did the early Egyptians explain events of nature?
2. Why did the early Egyptians worship animals?
3. What was the most important deity?
4. What cycles did the Egyptians observe in nature?
5. What inspired the invention of the first solar calendar?
6. Why did the Egyptians believe in an Afterlife?
7. What myth explains the miracle of rebirth?
8. What was Ma'at?
9. Why are Egyptian gods often depicted with animal heads and human bodies?
10. Describe a typical day in the life of a priest.
11. Who was Aten?
12. How did a temple of Aten differ from those of the traditional gods?
13. Describe the appearance of Akhenaten.
14. Who was Akhenaten's wife? Describe her appearance.

15. How did the Egyptian religion change after the death of Akhenaten?

Further Thoughts

1. The eye of Horus (also called the *wadjet* eye), is a symbol for health, and it is ever present in today's world. The familiar Rx that appears at the bottom of every doctor's prescription is derived from the symbol of Horus's eye. Can you see the major lines of the Rx below?

Eye of Horus.

2. Akhenaten's name was omitted from the lists of Egypt's pharaohs made by the priestly scribes who lived after him. His temple in Aketaten was disassembled, and the blocks were buried in the desert sands. This century, nearly 45,000 blocks from the temple (they are called talatats) have been uncovered, and computers have been used to match the blocks (many are inscribed with pictures and hieroglyphs) so that they can eventually be reassembled. So Akenaten's temple to the sun also will once again rise above the Nile Valley.

3. The Egyptians had two falcon-headed gods, Ra and Horus. If you have trouble telling them apart, remember that Ra had the sun disc on his head, and Horus wore the double crown.

The bust of Nefertiti

4. This beautiful bust of Nefertiti was discovered amid the ruins of a workshop in Amarna in 1912. It is made of painted limestone. It is one of the most copied works of ancient Egyptian art. It is now in the Egyptian Museum in Berlin.

Projects

1. Pretend that you are one of the earliest dwellers of the Nile Valley. There is no organized religion. You are fascinated and yet frightened by the apparent movement of the sun. Write a story that explains why the sun crosses the sky each day and then is replaced by the stars at night. Give free rein to your imagination. Illustrate your story, and then present it to your class.

2. Write a play based on the story of Osiris, Seth and Isis. Choose several classmates to act it out.

3. "To speak of the dead is to make them live again." This is a quote from the wall of an Egyptian tomb. Explain what it means.

4. Find out more about Egypt's ten or twelve most important deities. Draw a picture on poster board of each one and attach a short description of his/her special duties. Below is a drawing of Anubis, Thoth and the Devourer done by Ben Keyes, a seventh grade student at Fay School.

Anubis, Thoth and the Devourer. by Ben Keyes

CHAPTER 6

MUMMIES AND BURIAL

As we have seen, the earliest Nile dwellers buried their dead in shallow pits in the desert sand. Occasionally, when high winds blew the sand away from a grave or a scavenging animal dug up a dead body, the Egyptians were relieved to observe that the disinterred corpse still retained its skin, hair and nails. This is because the bacteria that cause decay thrive in moist conditions but cannot live in the dry desert. The sand actually absorbs moisture and is one of nature's best preservatives. Since death did not totally alter the basic structure of a human being, the Egyptians reasoned (or hoped) that once a person was buried beneath the surface of the ground, he might lead a second life in the Land of the Dead. This is why they placed tools, pottery and a supply of food in the grave when they buried someone.

The Ka and the Ba

The Egyptians believed that the human spirit had two distinct parts, known as the ka and the ba. The ka was a person's life force, his vital essence. It was represented in writing by two upraised arms. The god Khnum created a person's body as well as his ka by modeling them on his potter's wheel. He then placed them in the mother's womb to await birth. During life, the ka followed the person around like a shadow. When the person died, his ka was released, and it flew up to the heavens. The ba consisted of the personality traits that made a person unique. After the person died and was buried, his ba was transformed into a human-headed bird.

Every day the ba-bird flew off to visit the land of the living.

Both the ka and the ba returned to the dead body at night - to rest and prepare for the next day. So it was important that the body remain fairly intact. If something happened to the body, the ka and the ba would not be able to return and the person's spirit would be deprived of an Afterlife.

Ba bird.

Decay Within the Mastaba

During the early years of the Old Kingdom, the pharaohs were buried in flat mud-brick tombs called *mastabas*. (Ordinary people continued to be buried in shallow pits in the sand.) The cold, moist interior of the tombs caused the bodies to decay and rot as they never would in the simpler graves in the sand. Frequently, these tombs were broken into and robbed, and after such an event Egyptian priests entered the inner chamber to assess the damage. They were horrified to discover that the body had nearly disintegrated! They knew that the ka could not survive without an intact body to inhabit. Clearly, there was an urgent need to find a method to preserve a body in such a way that it could survive in a moist environment. But how could the corpses lying in massive brick tombs be made as impervious to decay as those of the common peasants buried beneath the sand?

A New Method of Preservation

The priests who supervised funeral proceedings began to experiment with different methods of preserving meat. Among the materials used in these experiments was natron, a mineral similar to salt that lined the dried lake beds (*wadis*) in the western desert. Imagine the excitement those early scientists must have felt when they discovered that by covering a piece of meat with a large quantity of natron they could slow down or even stop the process of decay! The natron dried out and thus preserved the meat just as effectively as the desert sand, and in a much shorter period of time. This discovery led to the development of a method of body preservation known as mummification.

The Egyptian priests who specialized in the preparation of royal noble bodies for burial were a small and elite group. They followed specific procedures that varied very little over a period of three thousand years. They did their work so efficiently that many of the bodies they prepared for burial are still well preserved. Some of them are on display in museums. We owe much of what we know about the mummification process to the writings of the Greek historian Herodotus. Upon his visit to Egypt in the 5th century B.C.E., he became fascinated by the procedure, and he wrote long descriptions of the steps followed by the embalmers.

How To Prepare A Mummy

The first step in preparing a body was to cut a small slit in the left side. The priests were reluctant to make the initial incision themselves, because the human body was considered sacred and it was sinful to cut the skin of another person. They resolved this dilemma by calling in a person whose sole profession was to make incisions in dead bodies. As soon as he made the cut, the fellow was ceremoniously chased away by the priests. They even threw stones at him! In this way, the priests were spared from performing a sinful act and yet enabled to work on the internal parts of the corpse. The men who made the incisions occupied a low status in society, being somewhat akin to the hangmen of medieval times. Yet, they were increasingly in demand as the mummification process was ordered by more noble families, so they were seldom idle.

Once the incision was made, the priests removed the liver, the lungs, the intestines, and the stomach from the body. They knew that these organs would begin to rot very quickly if something wasn't done about them. During the Old Kingdom the heart was left in place, but in later periods it was removed, preserved in natron, and then returned to the body. The Egyptians believed that the heart was the source of all thought and emotion and therefore considered it the most important organ.

The brain was removed in a rather grisly manner. A hook was pushed through the nostrils, breaking a membrane and penetrating the inner skull. Then the brain was pulled out in bits and pieces. Sometimes an acidic liquid was poured into the skull. The head was shaken vigorously and then the liquefied brain was poured out. The remnants of this organ were simply disposed of, since the Egyptians didn't consider the brain to be of any importance!

The next step in preparing a mummy was to wash the body cavity with wine (the Egyptians knew that alcohol inhibited decay). It was then brushed with sweet smelling spices to dull the odor of rotting flesh. Next the cavity was stuffed with natron wrapped in linen cloths, and then the entire body was covered with a blanket of natron to draw out the moisture. It lay upon a slanted board, the excess fluid dripping slowly into a container at the bottom of the board. The priests had to leave the corpse in its "natron bath" for a long time (about forty days), since the human body is over seventy-five percent water. As the fluid dripped out, the corpse shrank and became withered and leathery.

The four organs that had been removed were also dried in natron. Afterwards, they were wrapped in strips of linen and placed in four stone or ceramic jars called the Canopic Jars. The lids of the jars were sculpted to represent the heads of the four sons of Horus: Qebsenuef (a falcon), Hapi (a baboon), Duamutef (a jackal) and Imseti (a human). Each son protected a specific organ: the falcon guarded the intestines, the baboon protected the lungs, the jackal was in charge of the stomach, and the human took care of the liver. The jars were named after the Egyptian city of Canopus where Osiris was traditionally represented by a stone vase with a lid carved in the shape of his head. The organs had to be preserved in the jars so that in the Afterlife they could be magically reunited with the body.

Canopic jars.

After forty days, the dried out corpse was removed from the natron and washed with Nile water. It was brushed again with imported spices and oils to give it a pleasant smell and to prevent the skin from cracking. Then the cavity and the head were stuffed with linen cloths and sawdust to give them a more rounded and life-like shape. Wax, stones, or even onions were placed in the eye sockets. The incision made for the removal of the organs was sealed with resin (a sticky material similar to the sap of a tree), and a stone slate carved with the eye of Horus (the symbol of recovery and good heath) was placed over it. The arms were crossed, and often the fingernails and toenails were covered with caps of gold. Bracelets and a necklace of gold and precious stones were placed on the body. Then it was carefully wrapped with long strips of linen—the arms, legs, fingers and toes were wrapped individually.

Many layers of linen were added until the mummy seemed to be the size of a normal living human being (a pharaoh might have as many as eighty layers). Frequently, small figures and charms (amulets) were tucked between the layers of linen. Among these were small mummy-shaped figures called *shawabtis*. The Egyptians believed that these figures would magically come to life to serve the dead pharaoh or nobleman in the next world once his tomb was sealed. Shawabti means "answerer." These figures often carried hoes and baskets to use in the fields of the Land of the Dead. They were a practical improvement over the procedures of the very early dynasties when a king's servants were often sacrificed and buried with him!

During the New Kingdom the priests covered the layers of linen with resin to seal out moisture. Unfortunately, the resin turned black and became dry and brittle, making the mummy appear as though it had been burned on a funeral pyre. The word "mummy" comes from the Arabic word for resin (*momia*).

The head of the mummy was covered with a portrait mask. In most cases, the mask was made of cartonnage, a material similar to paper maché, although the mask of a pharaoh was made of gold. The purpose of the mask was to help the ka identify the body. Once the mask was in place, the entire mummy was covered with a cloth called a shroud and (during the New Kingdom) sealed again with resin. The mummy now closely resembled Osiris, although of course its face was not green.

The Egyptians were so successful as embalmers that many of the mummies survive intact to this day. Recently, the Boston Museum of Fine Arts sent several mummies to a Boston hospital where they were given a CT Scan (a kind of x-ray that reveals different layers of the body). Thanks to this modern process as well as powerful

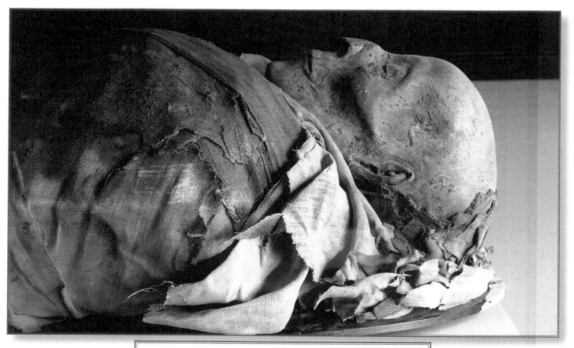

The well preserved face of an ancient Egyptian prince.

Coffin from the Middle Kingdom

electron microscopes and forensic tests, scientists have discovered a great deal about the people who died thousands of years ago without having to remove the linen coverings. For example, they have learned that one of the mummies had a gum abscess and hardening of the arteries. Several mummies had carbon in their lungs, which must have made them breathless and prone to severe coughing spells. The condition was probably caused by breathing the smoke of oil lamps and heating fires. Another mummy is wearing false teeth. Modern technology also makes it possible to detect blood groups and hereditary traits, thus making it possible to identify family connections among existing mummies.

The Coffin

Coffins changed somewhat during the three thousand years of Egypt's civilization. In the early days of the Old Kingdom, a mummy was buried lying on its side in a rectangular wooden box. Eyes were painted on the outside of the coffin. Were these to enable the mummy to see, or did they simply represent the health-restoring eye of Horus? We cannot be sure, but perhaps both possibilities apply. On the inside of

the coffin were paintings of food, tools, and even servants that were intended to come alive when the tomb was sealed. The box bore instructions for magic spells that the deceased needed to recite to ward off evil forces on his difficult journey to the Land of the Dead. The walls of the pyramids, the royal tombs of the Old Kingdom, were carved with similar instructions. Known as the Pyramid Texts, these writings describe a total of 750 different spells!

The coffins of the Middle Kingdom were sometimes shaped like people with their legs bound, like the mummies they contained. Each was painted with the idealized face and body of the deceased person and decorated with figures of the major deities associated with the dead—Isis and Nephthys, Ma'at, Anubis, and Osiris. The goddesses were often shown with outstretched wings, which were supposed to protect the ka.

During the New Kingdom, the mummies were placed in nests of mummy-shaped coffins that resemble modern sets of wooden Russian dolls. The coffin bearing the body fit into a larger coffin of similar design, which, in turn, fit into a still larger one. The three were then placed into a huge stone coffin called a sarcophagus. A papyrus scroll containing the same magic formulas as the earlier Pyramid Texts was also placed in the sarcophagus. Archaeologists refer to such a scroll as The Book of the Dead.

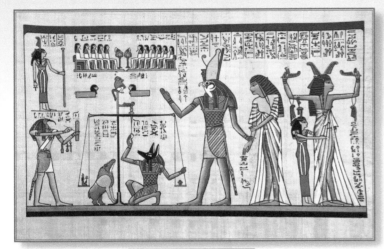

The Book of the Dead

The Journey to the Underworld

And what were the terrible obstacles that awaited the spirit of a deceased? The Egyptians believed that once the tomb was sealed, the spirit embarked upon a boat to ride across the tumultuous River of Death; on the western shore Osiris patiently awaited its arrival. The boat had to pass through twelve gates guarded by serpents. This was when all those magic spells came in handy! If it was lucky enough to make it to the western shore, the spirit had to defend itself at a trial where it was judged by forty-two gods. It had to swear that it had not committed any of a long list of sins. (One of the worst sins a farmer could commit was to build a dam across an irrigation canal.) To prove innocence, the heart of the deceased was weighed on a balance scale against a feather that symbolized goodness and truth (Ma'at). If the two sides balanced, the spirit was granted eternal life. It would dwell forever in the Fields of the Blessed, a replica of the Nile Valley minus the miseries of drought,

famine and physical suffering and enhanced by the presence of the gods. But if the heart was heavier than the feather, the wretched spirit would immediately be consumed by the Devourer, a horrible-looking creature that was part crocodile, part lion, and part hippopotamus (three of Egypt's deadliest animals). In The Book of the Dead, Anubis (the god of mummies and protector of the dead) is shown weighing the dead man's heart against the feather while Thoth, the ibis-headed god of wisdom and writing, records the verdict. Osiris, Isis and several other gods look on and await the verdict.

During the Old Kingdom, only royalty and the nobility could expect to have their bodies preserved as mummies. Over the years, however, a "proper burial" became available to anyone who could afford the very expensive procedures of mummification and tomb construction (more about that in the next chapter). Archaeologists have found the mummies of scribes, master craftsmen, and even a musician. And, as we have seen, such sacred animals as cats, bulls, baboons, and crocodiles were also mummified for the Afterlife.

The Funeral

Once a human mummy was prepared, it was escorted to its final resting place by a funeral procession. The coffin rode on a sled (resembling a boat, of course) that was pulled by oxen. Another smaller sled carried the Canopic Jars. Behind followed the family members, priests, servants and mourners, many of whom were paid to weep hysterically. When the procession arrived at the tomb, a priest wearing a mask of Anubis performed a final ceremony called the Opening of the Mouth. He touched the mouth of the mummy's mask with a special wand while chanting some magical words. This ritual enabled the ba to leave the physical body, so that it could visit the land of the living by day and unite with the ka in the tomb at night.

After the ceremony, the mummy was carried into the tomb and (in the later years) placed in the sarcophagus. The Canopic Jars, as well as many objects required in the Afterlife (furniture, tools, weapons, and jewelry) were carefully arranged in the tomb. Statues of the dead person were also placed there so that should something happen to the mummy (tomb robberies were all too common) the ka could reside in one of the stone figures. It was important the the name of the deceased be written down on the coffin and on the walls - the more times the better - to help the ba and the ka find their way back to the tomb at night.

The Mortuary Temple

Outside of the tomb was a shrine with an altar. After the burial, the subjects of a pharaoh or the relatives of a high-ranking official were expected to bring offerings of food and place them on the altar for the ka. The ka could consume the essence of these offerings - the priests are the ones who actually ate the food, since it was of no use to the dead. There was a false door (a carving of a door) in the wall through which the ka was expected to enter the shrine. The walls of the shrines were also decorated with paintings of food, which would become real when a priest recited the appropriate magical words. Of course, even ordinary people needed to make offerings at the burial places of their deceased loved ones. In the New Kingdom, it was not unusual for a family to enjoy a pleasant picnic by the altar, sharing their experiences and happy times with the ka of their departed relative!

Although the Egyptians devoted a good deal of time to planning for death, we should not conclude that they were a morbid and gloomy race. To the contrary, they were so content with the quality of their everyday lives that they wanted them to go on forever, in this world and the next.

Questions

1. How were the early Egyptian bodies preserved?
2. What were the ka and the ba?
3. What was the major drawback of a mastaba?
4. What is natron?
5. Why did the priests chase away the man who made the incision in the body?
6. What did the Egyptians consider the center of human thought and emotion?
7. What were the Canopic Jars?
8. What was a shawabti?
9. Describe the journey to the Underworld.
10. What was the function of the mortuary temple?

Further Thoughts

1. Many of the mummies buried in ancient Egypt were torn apart and destroyed by tomb robbers seeking the priceless jewelry and amulets wrapped within the layers of linen. Only the foot of the mighty Pharaoh Khufu remained in his tomb after

it was plundered! In the nineteenth century, thanks to the discovery of the riches of Egypt by Napoleon, European archaeologists and ordinary fortune hunters gathered up mummies and shipped them to England and France. There they were bought by wealthy people who found it entertaining to pass an evening with friends unwrapping an Egyptian mummy. Once the mummy was exposed to the air, it began to break apart and disintegrate. This was a sad ending for a once powerful king or noble. Some mummies were even ground up and sold in bottles that advertised their miraculous medicinal powers!

2. The mummy of Ramses II has been unwrapped and examined directly. Scientists have discovered that the boastful pharaoh was only five feet six inches tall. He had red hair and his face was pockmarked. He died in his eighties of arterial sclerosis. In 1977, Egyptian authorities discovered that the 3,000-year-old mummy was being consumed by a fungus. Ramses was sent to France to be treated. The mummy was given a passport that listed his occupation as "king— deceased!" In Paris the mummy was treated with radiation and cured of its affliction.

3. During the New Kingdom, priests from Thebes removed many mummies from tombs that had been robbed or violated and placed them for safety's sake in a deep shaft in a cliff face. These were discovered in 1881 and transported by the Egyptian Antiquities Service to the Cairo Museum. The customs duty officer at the city gates classified these priceless objects as dried fish!

4. Since the ka consumed only the essence of the food, it could gain sustenance if someone simply thought about an offering. This is borne out by the phrase found carved on the walls of many tombs: "Oh you, who live on earth and pass by this stele [grave marker], if you love life and hate death, say: may he receive a thousand loaves of bread and a thousand jugs of beer!

Projects

1. Mummify a piece of meat. Fill a large dish with salt. Place a thin slice of beef in the dish, and scoop the salt over it until it is covered. Examine the meat every day, making certain that it is covered with salt when you return it to the dish. After a few days, all the moisture will have been removed. The beef has been preserved, and it will last for a long time. Keep it in a dry place, and nibble on it whenever you are hungry!

2. Pretend that you are an artist and that you are painting the walls of your own tomb (or the sides of your wooden coffin). On a piece of paper, draw the kinds of food that you would like to be able to enjoy forever. On another piece of paper, draw yourself performing the activities that you would like to do for eternity. On a third piece of paper, draw servants doing the kinds of things that would have to be done but that you wouldn't want to do yourself in the next life.

CHAPTER 7

TOMBS AND TEMPLES

As we learned in the last chapter, the earliest tombs constructed for the pharaohs were mastabas—rectangular, flat-topped structures made of mud brick. (Mastaba means "bench" in Arabic.) A mastaba's burial chamber was cut into the rock below the

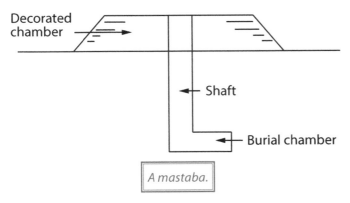

A mastaba.

ground. The body of the deceased was placed in a wooden coffin and lowered into this chamber through an opening in the roof. On the upper level was a larger chamber with walls decorated with paintings of various aspects of the dead person's life. It was into this chamber that family members and priests came to offer prayers for the deceased and to leave food for his ka. Many of these tombs can be visited today at Saqqara (near Cairo) and Abydas (near Thebes).

The Innovations of Imhotep

In the early years of the Old Kingdom, a pharaoh named Djoser noticed that the brick in the mastabas gradually crumbled over time. He was determined to have a final resting place that would last. He called upon his chief architect and vizier, a talented man named Imhotep, to design a more permanent tomb. After all, the Egyptian word for tomb means "house for eternity." Imhotep was a man of many talents. He is the first scientist in history that we know by name; his work so impressed the Egyptians that later, in the New Kingdom, he was worshipped as the god of medicine. But it is his skill as an architect that concerns us here.

Imhotep rejected the traditional mud bricks and built Djoser's tomb entirely of stone. His design was unique: First he built a square mastaba, and then on top of that he built another, smaller one. He repeated the process until he had a total of six mastabas, one on top of the other, rising over two hundred feet in the air. The tomb looked like a giant staircase, and it is known to this day as the Step Pyramid. There is a theory that the steps were supposed to symbolize the pharaoh's ascent to the heavens where he could join the sun god Ra. Underground chambers and passages were decorated with relief (carved) paintings of Djoser performing religious rites.

Imhotep added smaller structures around the tomb, including a chapel on the

The Step Pyramid

northern side into which the priests would bring their offerings of food and drink for Djoser's ka. A false door was cut partway through the wall between the tomb and the chapel for the ka to enter and receive its food. Around the central tomb were later built stone mastabas of the nobles who were closest to the pharaoh. Surrounding the entire complex was a high wall of limestone over one mile in perimeter.

Djoser's tomb is the earliest example of a stone monument built on a grand scale. It marks the beginning of the era of pyramid tombs in Egypt.

Bigger and Better Tombs

The kings that came after Djoser saw the advantages of stone tombs and ordered the construction of ever larger and more magnificent structures for their own Afterlives. Whereas Imhotep had used small rocks (because they were easy to work with), the later architects ordered considerably larger rocks that were cut in quarries along the Nile.

Pharaoh Sneferu's step pyramid was much larger than Djoser's. Furthermore, the steps were filled in with rubble so that the structure had the smooth appearance of a true pyramid. Upon its completion, the entire surface was covered with a facing of white limestone. It must have gleamed majestically in the desert sunlight. Part of the facing is currently being restored.

Not all pyramid designs succeeded. One tomb is known as the Bent Pyramid. The angle of its sides was so steep that the original plan had to be dramatically altered when the structure was half built. Otherwise, it would have been outrageously

tall, resembling an inverted ice cream cone! As a result of this adjustment in design, the pyramid rises to a certain height and then the sides bend slightly inward toward a more modest summit. It remains a colossal example of poor planning!

The Bent Pyramid

Eighty-seven pyramids of the Old Kingdom survive to this day. They line the edge of the desert on the western bank of the Nile. (Remember, the western horizon was considered the entrance to the Land of the Dead.)

The Great Pyramid of Giza

The greatest pyramid of all was built by Sneferu's successor, Khufu (called Cheops by the Greeks). Sited on the rocky plateau of Giza not far from Saqqara, this massive structure required the labor of thousands of Egyptian peasants working for about twenty years. The base of the pyramid measures 775 feet on each side and it covers an area of thirteen acres. That is the equivalent of twelve football fields! It rises 481 feet, about the height of a forty-story building. Known as the Great Pyramid, it is the only remaining Wonder of the Ancient World. Khufu's tomb contains over two and a half million blocks of granite and limestone. When Napoleon was in Egypt, he speculated that the stones used to build the Great Pyramid could form a wall around France ten feet high and one foot thick!

Preparing the ground properly for the base of such a massive structure was essential. If the surface was not absolutely flat, the entire pyramid would collapse. The Egyptians knew that the surface of water is always level. So they dug a system of trenches criss-crossing the area of the base of the pyramid and then flooded the trenches, marking the water line on the sides. When the trenches were drained, the workers leveled the ground to the marks left by the water. Then they filled in the trenches with dirt and sand. The result was a base that was completely flat, parallel to the horizon. (The southeast corner of the Great Pyramid is only a half inch higher than the northwest corner.)

Base of the Great Pyramid

The building of the pyramid required great technical skill. The rocks had to be measured and cut precisely. Then they were placed in such a way that the four sides of Khufu's tomb are within a few centimeters of being equal. The architect used basic principles of geometry to determine the correct angle of slant, the four sides arising from the square base and coming to a point at the top. The slightest error in the angle of incline would have resulted in a substantial misalignment of the four sides at the apex. Eighty percent of the mass of the pyramid is at its base, and this makes it a very sturdy structure.

Most of the building was done during the Inundation when farming came to a halt, although skilled stone-masons probably worked throughout the year. The laborers were paid in bread, barley and beer. There is no record of complaining on the part of the builders of the royal tombs. After all, they were toiling on behalf of the divine pharaoh. But one thing is clear. Such an ambitious undertaking as the construction of a pyramid could never have been achieved if Egypt were not an extremely stable and prosperous country whose leaders had a genius for organization.

Obtaining the Building Blocks

The bulk of the Great Pyramid consists of huge blocks of granite that were quarried about six hundred miles up the Nile from Giza near the First Cataract. It was no easy task for the workers to cut the blocks out of the rock cliffs since they had only primitive copper tools. Rising to the challenge, the Egyptians devised a procedure that, although arduous, was very effective. First they drew

Pyramid Entrance

marks on the rock to outline each block; then they chipped small slits in the rock along the outlines with copper chisels and wooden mallets. The next step was to hammer wedge-shaped pieces of wood into the slits. When water was poured over the wood it swelled, causing the rock to crack along the outlines. The workers then used their chisels and mallets to break apart the rock along the cracks. Once a block was cut from the rock, it was hauled away with ropes (made of woven papyrus reeds) and wooden levers. Finally, its rough edges were chiseled until the six sides were perfectly square.

Small armies of laborers dragged the blocks on wooden sleds to a barge waiting at the bank of the Nile. While the strongest workers strained every muscle pulling the ropes attached to the sleds, others placed a series of logs in their path in order to keep the sleds from sinking into the sand. A third group threw oil or water (and in some cases goats' milk) under the advancing sled to reduce friction. The blocks were extremely heavy, each weighing about two and a half tons. Modern scientists have estimated that ten strong men were required to pull one block of granite. The gangs of workers had their own identifying nicknames (such as "the hardworking gang"), and they often cut these epithets into the blocks of stone they handled. The markings are still legible.

Because the Nile was in flood, the barges bearing the granite blocks could dock close to the site of the pyramid at the edge of the desert. Workers unloaded the blocks onto sleds and dragged them to the construction site. Other laborers hauled them on wooden rollers up ramps of earth and rubble that coiled around the sides of the pyramid. It must have been back-breaking work to drag the blocks up the ramps. How much easier it would have been had the Egyptians known about pulleys and cranes. Each block was placed in position in a bed of mortar made of sand, lime and water. Once the granite core of the pyramid was completed, a limestone capstone was placed at the very top. This was a pointed stone covered with gold. It was shaped into a plug at the base so that it fit neatly into a hole in the top layer of granite. Then the workers reversed their direction, covering the granite with an outer shell of gleaming white limestone. As they retreated downward, the workers removed the ramps. At last they reached the base, and the pyramid was complete.

Inside the pyramid the workers left room for a maze of passages and a central chamber where the Pharaoh's coffin and treasures were placed. The architect apparently changed his plans for the location of the chamber two times.

Outer Structures

A temple on the eastern side of the pyramid had a sanctuary where the priests could offer food and drink to Khufu's ka. A causeway ran from this temple to a smaller temple near the edge of the river, the site of the ceremony of the Opening of the Mouth. Later, smaller pyramids were built beside the Pharaoh's tomb for his many queens. This century archaeologists discovered a disassembled funereal boat in a pit near the Great Pyramid. Its function was to carry Khufu's ka to the Land of the Dead. (Apparently it would be magically put together again in the Afterlife.) This vessel has been reassembled in modern times and is exhibited in a museum erected next to the pyramid. Scientists using laser technology have also discovered other boats that were buried around the tomb. They photographed one of them by driving a long pole mounted with a tiny camera into the buried chamber.

This method enabled them to learn much about the ancient craft without physically disturbing it.

Khufu's funereal boat

The Other Pyramids of Giza

Khufu's son Khafre (his Greek name is Chefren) built a smaller pyramid, but he tried to make it look as large as his father's tomb by building it on a raised layer of rock. Khafre's successor, Menkaure (Mycerinus), built a third pyramid, smaller still. The three pyramids at Giza stand majestically as a testament to the sophisticated engineering skills and the organizing genius of the Egyptians of the Old Kingdom. They still put on quite a show. Their stone surfaces dramatically change color in a twenty-four hour cycle, appearing silver in the moonlight, gray at dawn, gold at noon, and rose in the sunset.

Khafre's pyramid still has some of the original limestone casing near its top. The casing stones fit so tightly that it is impossible to slip a sheet of paper between any two of them.

The three pyramids of Giza

The Sphinx

Near Khafre's pyramid is a massive statue known as the Sphinx. It has the body of a lion with the head (archaeologists believe) of Khafre, and it appears to be guarding the three pyramids of Giza. Historians believe that it was carved from an outcropping of rock and the rubble left over from the construction of Khafre's tomb. The Sphinx is the largest surviving statue from ancient times, measuring 190 feet in length and 66 feet in height. It was originally painted with bright colors. Perhaps the human head represents wisdom while the lion body stands for strength (and royalty).

Storytellers of the New Kingdom often told how the Sphinx was uncovered from the drifting sands that had nearly swallowed it up. According to their tale, a young prince who would later become Thutmose IV was passing through Giza, and he decided to take a nap near the three pyramids. (By the New Kingdom the pyramids were already considered a part of ancient history!) While he slept, he dreamed that the Sphinx told him that he would soon become king if he dug it out of the sand. When he awoke, Thutmose immediately gathered an army of workers to shovel the sand from the statue. When he became pharaoh (he didn't have to wait long), he inscribed a tall granite stone (called a *stele*) with the story of his dream and had it placed between the paws of the Sphinx. Remnants of the stele are still there.

For centuries after the decline of ancient Egypt the Sphinx was again half buried

The Sphinx

Close-up view of the Sphinx

by the drifting dunes. Actually, the sand protected it from winds and air-borne particles. Since being uncovered in the nineteenth century, the stone has been slightly worn by wind erosion, and exposure to the polluted air of modern times has caused even more serious damage to the outer surfaces. Plans are underway to repair the cracks and crevices in the huge stone monument.

The Inner Wall Paintings

The interiors of the pyramids are of great interest to historians. Paintings on the walls of corridors and chambers depict the most important aspects of the lives of the deceased and hence tell us a great deal about the culture of the Old Kingdom. As we know, the Egyptians were so content with their existence along the Nile that they hoped for an Afterlife that would be similar to it in every way (with the added advantage of living in the presence of the gods). They

believed that the paintings in their tombs would magically become reality once the priests had chanted some secret words and the doors were sealed. There are hunting and boating scenes as well as pictures of peasants laboring in the fields. In the Afterlife, these peasants would supposedly serve the pharaoh. And there are drawings of all kinds of food—bread, fruit, fish, pieces of meat, and wine—that were to provide the pharaoh's ka with sustenance throughout eternity.

The stylized (and unrealistic) manner of Egyptian painting varied little for three thousand years, with the exception of the reign of Akhenaten. At first it might appear that the Egyptians were rather poor artists, since they drew people as they are viewed from the side and the front at the same time. The head is always shown in profile, and yet the eye is presented full face; the legs are viewed from the side while the torso is turned toward the viewer.

Inner walls of tomb of Ramses VI

The Egyptians adopted this odd way of painting people in positions that are clearly a physical impossibility because it enabled them to reveal the most about an individual. The side view of the face shows the person's unique profile, while the front view of the eyes most effectively displays the color of the iris. A side view of the legs shows a specific movement while a front view of the torso allows the artist to make clear what both arms are doing. Nor are paintings of objects true-to-life. Typically a picture of a box shows both the exterior of the container as well as the objects that lie within it. This is not so surprising when we realize that an important purpose of such a painting was to record the possessions of the deceased.

The Case Against Creative Expression

The tomb paintings are proportionately very exact. To accomplish this precision of form the artist always prepared the surface of a wall with a grid of small squares. He made the lines in the following way. He attached one end of a string to the ceiling, covered the string with red paint, and then, holding the other end near the floor directly below where it was attached at the ceiling, he snapped it against the wall like the string of a bow. Once he had marked the vertical lines in this manner, he attached the string to different carefully measured places up from floor to ceiling and made the horizontal lines. The result was a well-defined grid of guidelines that enabled him to sketch his figures in the strict proportions dictated by tradition. For tens of centuries, every major figure in an Egyptian painting occupied a specific number of squares. For example, a standing figure measured eighteen vertical squares, while a human hand filled one square. Minor figures, such as wives, children and servants, were represented on a significantly smaller scale.

Egyptian artists did not question the rigid rules of their teachers. Innovative techniques such as foreshortening a limb to indicate perspective (making a painting more realistic) were never considered (except, of course, at the time of Akhenaten). The artists feared that if they strayed from the traditional standards, their paintings would lose their magical qualities and the deceased would be denied the opportunity for an Afterlife. A pharaoh or nobleman felt desperately dependent upon the skill and precision of the artists who painted his tomb. This helps to explain why the painters never displayed the slightest originality in their work. They couldn't take any chances. They were technicians, not poets.

Egyptian Statues

The statues found in the tombs and temples of the Old Kingdom similarly reflect the unbending discipline of the Egyptian artists. The pose is always the same. The men

A typical statue

stand stiffly with the left foot forward while the women have their feet more closely together. The skin of the men was painted red, perhaps to reflect the fact that the men spent a lot of time in the hot sun, while the skin of the women was a pale yellow. Every face wears an expression of serene aloofness, and it is difficult to distinguish one person from another. As we know, the statues were of great importance in the magic of the Afterlife, since they provided a substitute resting place for the ka, should anything happen to the mummy. Sculptors were, in fact, among the most richly rewarded of artists.

Theft and Vandalism in the Royal Tombs

It is a sad commentary that all of the pyramids of the Old Kingdom were robbed.

Priceless statues, jewels, and furniture are long gone, and even the mummies have been violated. The limestone facing that gave those huge monuments a clean, gleaming white appearance in the hot desert sun has mostly disappeared, leaving the rough granite stones exposed. Actually, many of the buildings of Cairo contain limestone removed from the pyramids of Giza. Nor has the Sphinx remained intact. During the nineteenth century some of Napoleon's soldiers used Khafre's nose for target practice and blew it off! Recent environmental pollution has caused many of the tomb wall paintings to deteriorate. Fortunately, copies were made of them by nineteenth and twentieth century artists, and these have become invaluable records.

As we learned earlier, the end of the Old Kingdom witnessed a trend toward building smaller tombs of mud-brick for king and government official alike. Pepi II was the last pharaoh to have a pyramid built. The construction and upkeep of the huge stone tombs had proven too much of a drain on the national economy, and besides, it had become clear that even those massive monuments were not impervious to theft.

The Valley of the Kings and the Valley of the Queens

During the Middle Kingdom, many nobles ordered their tombs to be cut into the rocky cliffs rising above the west bank of the Nile. When the capital was moved to Thebes in the New Kingdom, the pharaohs followed this trend in the construction of underground tombs. West of Thebes at the desert's edge there stretches a range of low mountains. Hidden behind the first row of

The Valley of the Kings

foothills are two quiet valleys that became the new royal cemeteries, known to us as the Valley of the Kings and the Valley of the Queens.

The tombs that were cut into the rock in the valleys were large and impressive. They contained high corridors and roomy chambers decorated with brilliant colors. As we have learned, the first pharaoh to be buried in this bleak and desolate setting was Thutmose I. The tomb of Seti I (the father of Ramses II) is the longest and most beautifully decorated burial site ever constructed in the Valley of the Kings. It consists of a series of rooms and corridors that gradually descend by means of numerous staircases hundreds of feet into the ground.

King Tut's Tomb

Although the tomb entrances were carefully hidden and the temples associated with them were placed a considerable distance away, such efforts to prevent robberies were in vain. The only royal tomb of this period that has been discovered nearly intact is that of King Tutankhamon,

popularly known as "King Tut." He was married to Ankhesenamon, a daughter of Akhenaten, and he came to power after the death of that eccentric king.

Tutankhamon's tomb was robbed once soon after it was sealed shut, but apparently the thieves were caught in the act, and the tomb was resealed. Two centuries later a new tomb was dug nearby, and the workmen

The golden mask

shoveled stone chips and rubble into the entrance to Tutankhamon's tomb. In this way, his tomb was hidden and protected until the twentieth century.

In 1922 a British archaeological expedition led by Howard Carter and financed by Lord Carnarvon discovered the tomb by accident. Their workers had been digging around the newer tomb when they suddenly uncovered a step leading to Tutankhamon's grave. Immediately they began to dig away the rubble, and they made their way down the steps to the door of the tombs. The seal was still intact. Once the seal had been dramatically broken, Carter was gripped with emotion as he peered into the chamber of the tomb. Asked if he could see anything, he gasped, "Yes, wonderful things!" The room was packed with thousands of priceless objects, including a golden throne decorated with a painting of Akhenaten and Nefertiti, a disassembled

The golden throne

chariot, carved wooden chests inlaid with gold, alabaster jars filled with perfumed oil, an ancient board game called Senet, boxes of preserved food (the young king apparently had a taste for roast duck), pine scented after-shave lotion, and even a flyswatter made from ostrich plumes! The mummy lay in a solid gold coffin within a stone sarcophagus that weighed 2,500 pounds! Painted on one of the walls of the tomb were the words, "I am yesterday, I know tomorrow."

Although Tutankhamon was a minor pharaoh (he died at the age of eighteen or nineteen), the discovery of his tomb has provided invaluable evidence of the great wealth and artistic accomplishments of the Egyptians of the New Kingdom. All of the objects placed in the tomb for use by the young pharaoh in his Afterlife now occupy an entire wing in the Cairo Museum, although the body still rests in his tomb in the Valley of the Kings.

Inner coffin and mummy of King Tut

The statue of Anubis that was guarding King Tut's coffin.

Temples of the New Kingdom

The tombs that honeycomb the valleys west of Thebes tell us much about the lives of the ancient Egyptians. Yet, it is the temples of the New Kingdom that represent the greatest architectural achievements of the period. There were two kinds of temples: cultus (for the worship of a deity) and mortuary (for the worship of a dead person). Many examples of each type have survived. Their vast dimensions reflect the grandiose ideals of the pharaohs of imperial Egypt.

Amon became the most important god of Thebes. During the New Kingdom, two magnificent temples were dedicated to him: one at Karnak to the north of the city, and the other at Luxor to the south. Once a year, a golden statue of Amon mounted on an elaborate sacred barge slowly proceeded up the Nile from the sanctuary at Karnak to the temple at Luxor. Known as the festival of Opet, this was an occasion for music and merry-making as well as religious ceremonies. And, of course, it gave the local people a rare opportunity to view the sacred statue.

The cult of Amon eventually merged with that of the traditional sun god of all of Egypt, Ra. The new composite god, Amon-Ra, was to remain Egypt's major deity until the end of the first century B.C.E.

The Temple At Karnak

Karnak was, in fact, a complex of temples, shrines and ceremonial halls covering about one square mile, but the largest structure was the Great Temple of Amon. Since Amon had become an important deity, every pharaoh tried to please him by adding to the temple built in his honor. Unfortunately, they often tore down the works of their

Ruins of the Karnak temple complex

Ruins of the Hypostyle Hall at Karnak

Since the pharaohs were constantly building their own pylons to the temple at Karnak, it now has ten! Between two of these lie the ruins of the Hypostyle Hall, the largest columned hall in the world: It covers 54,000 square feet. The hall was begun by Seti I and completed by his son, Ramses II. Some of the stone blocks used for it were removed from Akhenaten's temple. The roof is supported by l34 beautifully decorated stone columns. The 12 columns of the central section of the hall are 69 feet high and measure 12 feet in diameter. One hundred people can easily stand atop each one. The capitals (top sections) of the inner columns are carved and painted as papyrus plants in flower. The flowering papyrus was a symbol of life since it opened in response to the warmth and light of the sun god, Amon. The capitals of the outer columns are painted as the closed buds of the papyrus plant; they represent

predecessors and used those stones for their own structures. The temple was continually rebuilt and enlarged for hundreds of years, so that today its ruins make it the largest standing house of worship in the world. It covers a vast five acres.

As we learned earlier, every Egyptian temple (regardless of size) conformed to the same basic design. An imposing pylon (gateway) opened onto one or several courtyards. Beyond, a long walkway lined with decorated pillars led to the sanctuary wherein resided the sacred statue of the god. At Karnak, an impressive avenue of 120 stone curly-horned ram-headed sphinxes (each holding a statue of Ramses II between its front paws) leads from a canal to the entrance to Amon's temple. During the New Kingdom, prisoners and booty of war were paraded in a royal procession along this avenue and presented to Amon.

Carved pillars at the temple at Karnak

The Temple of Hatshepsut

nature sleeping while the sun god visits the Land of the Dead. There are columns in other parts of the temple whose capitals depict the lotus flower. Like the papyrus, the lotus was a symbol of life and regeneration, for its blossoms also opened each morning in response to the light of the sun god. It has been suggested that every Egyptian temple represented the original island of creation that arose from the waters of Chaos: The columns shaped like palms, papyrus and lotus symbolize the primeval vegetation.

It is a wonder that the Egyptian workmen using very simple bronze tools could construct the rows of gigantic columns at Karnak. How did they do it? First, they placed the chiseled stone bases upon a flattened surface. They filled in the spaces between them with sand. A second layer of stone was then placed upon each base, and the edges were chiseled so that the two pieces of each column appeared to be joined. Then more sand was added. This procedure was repeated over and over again until the columns reached the desired height. An earthen ramp was constantly added to as the structures grew higher. At last the roof could be positioned over the columns. The final step was to carve and paint the columns. As the artists worked their way down from top to bottom, the ramp and sand were gradually removed.

The columns of the Hypostyle Hall are covered with hieroglyphs that tell many

Detail of the top of a column

stories about the Egyptian gods. The roof is painted dark blue and decorated with stars to suggest the heavens above the Nile Valley. Originally the hall was lighted by small windows located just under the roof. These are known as clerestory windows, and the Egyptians invented them. Clerestory windows have been used to bring light into large buildings, such as churches and museums, ever since ancient Egyptian times.

The temple of Luxor is connected to that of Karnak by an avenue of human-headed sphinxes. Unlike Karnak, Luxor was not added on to, and so it has an unspoiled simplicity that the grander temple lacks. The pylon (built by Ramses II) is covered with hieroglyphs describing the great king's "victory" over the Hittites at Kadesh. Four colossal statues of Ramses (two standing and two seated) originally flanked the gateway.

Hatshepsut, Egypt's great woman pharaoh, ordered a mortuary temple built at Deir el Bahri near the Valley of the Kings. This magnificent temple—which is actually a series of huge terraces—is cut into the rock with such artistry that the outer pillars seem to blend with the lines of the cliff itself. Originally, the myrrh trees she imported from Punt lined the temple walkways.

Ceremonial Obelisks

An obelisk is a tall, free-standing stone pillar topped by a pyramid-like point. It is cut from a single block of granite. Obelisks were placed in front of temples and carved with hieroglyphs boasting of the deeds and exploits of various pharaohs. Every pharaoh in the New Kingdom ordered obelisks built in his honor that were larger than those of his predecessors. Queen Hatshepsut had one

Egyptian obelisk in Paris

built that is 96 feet high. It's not surprising that Ramses II, that great egotist, had more obelisks built than all the others combined. Furthermore, he ordered the names of former kings rubbed off their obelisks and his own name chiseled in. He wanted to take credit for everything!

Today, few obelisks remain in Egypt, but there are over fifty of the ancient structures that have been transported to cities in Europe and America. The one standing at the center of the Place de la Concord in Paris comes from Amon's temple at Karnak.

Ramses' Temple At Abu Simbel

Ramses II had seven temples built along the Nile. The most famous one was cut into a sandstone cliff one hundred miles upstream from the First Cataract at Abu Simbel in Nubia. Although this temple was

Temple at Abu Simbel

and Ramses' temple was in danger of being flooded by the lake created by the backup of water. People from all parts of the world contributed $40 million to move the temple. This was an ambitious undertaking, given the size of the temple. It is 102 feet high. Each of the seated Ramses statues weighs 1200 tons, and the lips of each figure are three feet wide. This is how they did it. The statues and the temple itself were carefully sawed into large blocks, lifted by huge cranes to the top of a high cliff and then reassembled. Today the temple stands high above the waters of Lake Nasser, safe for future generations to enjoy and appreciate. Ramses would have been pleased.

supposedly dedicated to Amon, Ptah, Horus Harakhte (a composite god of Horus and Ra) and the goddess Hathor, it is really another of Ramses' tributes to his own greatness. Outside the temple are four colossal statues (67 feet high) of the seated Pharaoh (who else?). Inside are two pillared hallways decorated with descriptions of Ramses' bravery at his favorite battle, Kadesh. There are eight more statues of the Pharaoh within the temple. Every year on February 20th and October 20th a ray of sunlight penetrates the 160 foot corridor and falls upon the statues of the Amon and Ramses in the inner chapel. Perhaps Ramses designed the temple to glorify his thirty-year jubilee, which fell on October 20 (1260 B.C.E.).

In 1968, a dam was built just below Abu Simbel,

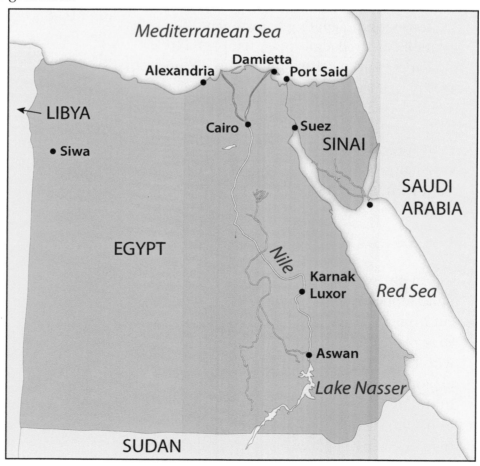

Questions

1. Why did Imhotep build Djoser's tomb out of stone?

2. What was the basic flaw in the design of the Bent Pyramid?

3. How did the Egyptian engineers prepare a flat base for Khufu's pyramid?

4. How did the Egyptian workers cut the blocks of granite?

5. Describe the Sphinx.

6. Why did the tomb painters shun innovation and spontaneity in their works?

7. Where is the Valley of the Kings?

8. Why was King Tut's tomb not destroyed by robbers?

9. How were the columns of the great temples constructed?

10. How was Ramses' temple at Abu Simbel rescued?

Further Thoughts

1. Connected with the discovery of King Tut's tomb is the story of the "Pharaoh's Curse." Lord Carnarvon died less than half a year after the discovery of the tomb from an infected mosquito bite that caused blood poisoning. According to the newspapers of the time, all the lights of Cairo momentarily went out when he died. Furthermore, his son in England stated that at the moment of his demise Carnarvon's dog howled and dropped dead! Others involved with the expedition died within a few years of the discovery of the tomb, and a friend of Carnarvon's died one day after visiting Tut's tomb. Some people said that these "mysterious" events offered proof that Carnarvon's forced entry into the tomb resulted in the curse of King Tut. Actually, Lord Carnarvon had been in poor health for some time, and his death was no surprise to his doctors. The other occurrences were simply coincidental in their timing. However, headlines about the "Pharaoh's Curse" sold a great many newspapers!

2. Modern technology is making it possible to locate many tombs that have been long buried by the desert sands. In Saqqara hundreds of hidden chambers have been detected by a sonar survey and have yet to be uncovered and studied. Some discoveries are made by accident. In 1989 seepage from a sewer line was threatening the foundation of a temple. When the authorities conducted an inspection of the soil in the temple courtyard, they discovered an ancient statue buried in the ground. They then dug further and unearthed twenty-four statues dating from the time of Amonhotep III (1391-53). The statues were in excellent condition, and they were very large (one was eight feet tall).

3. Archaeologists have recently uncovered the entire town of Deir el Medina near the Valley of the Kings. It was founded during the rule of Thutmose I, and was inhabited by the workmen who built and decorated the royal tombs. Many artifacts have been found there among the remains of the houses themselves that offer a detailed account of the everyday lives of the common people of the New Kingdom.

4. Tomb robberies were common occurrences in ancient Egypt. In many cases, a tomb robber would plot with a workman who had built the tomb, a guard, or even a priest or embalmer, and then he would split the loot with him! Tomb robbing often

became a family business, and descriptions of secret entrances were passed on from generation to generation. Sometimes the robbers would set the mummies on fire; these giant torches provided lighting for their looting! The treasure hunters of more recent times also did a great deal of damage. One used a battering ram to smash through blocked passages, destroying objects placed behind the doors. Fortunately, the Egyptian government has set up an agency to protect and preserve local antiquities.

4. Because of their reverence for traditions, the Egyptian artists of the first millennium B.C.E. painted exactly like the people had who lived three thousand years earlier. Find some illustrations of paintings from other cultures dating around 1000 B.C.E. and compare them with Egyptian art.

Projects

1. Using clay or paper maché, make a model of one of the great pyramids. Be sure to include the temples, smaller pyramids of the queens, mastabas of the nobles, and the causeway leading to the Nile.

2. Find out more about the tools used to construct the pyramids. An excellent source of information is David Macaulay's book *PYRAMID*. Write a short report.

3. The Great Pyramid is the only surviving Wonder of the Ancient World. Find out what the other six "wonders" were, and write a short report (with illustrations, if possible).

CHAPTER 8

SCIENCE AND MATH

The early Egyptians closely observed nearly every aspect of their natural environment, but they were especially intrigued by the heavens. Viewed through the clear, dry air of the desert, the evening stars glistened brightly against a background of blue-black. The Egyptians noticed that at particular times of year many of the stars came together in patterns. The more imaginative star-gazers could see shapes of animals outlined by these groups of stars. Shapes or images outlined by stars are called constellations. The Egyptians, of course, saw celestial outlines of the beasts that thrived in the Nile Valley; just as we identify the Big Dipper at night, they looked for the crocodile, the hippopotamus and the ox. While viewing the constellations they also noticed that certain sources of light (the planets) were always in motion while others (circumpolar stars that seem to revolve around the North Pole) never disappeared beyond the horizon. And others disappeared and reappeared at specific time intervals.

Measuring Time

As early as 3000 B.C.E. the Egyptians recognized the star Sirius (also known as the dog star), which appeared brighter than the other heavenly bodies. Its pattern was not as orderly as the other stars. Sometimes it would vanish, only to suddenly reappear one day for a short time. Then it would vanish again, and reappear the next day, this time shining in the heavens for a slightly longer period than the day before. This went on for several days until suddenly Sirius was gone,

not to be seen again for a long time. The Nile dwellers studied the strange phenomenon and noticed that Sirius always returned just before the river began to overflow its banks. From this observation they eventually realized that they could predict the onset of the flood by observing the star. And so Sirius became the harbinger of the Inundation. This advance warning enabled the farmers to harvest the last of their crops and to move their belongings and animals to higher ground before the river overflowed its banks.

To keep track of the daylight hours the Egyptians designed a shadow clock similar to a modern sundial. They also invented a water clock—a conical clay or stone bowl with a hole in the bottom through which water dripped at a specific rate. Lines on the inside of the bowl marked the twenty-four hours of the day as the water level slowly dropped.

One star is brightest

The First Solar Calendar

It turns out that Sirius makes its dramatic first appearance in the evening sky above Egypt every 365 1/4 days (precisely the time it takes the earth to revolve around the sun). By making a connection between Sirius and the Inundation, the Egyptians were able to create the world's first solar calendar. They had previously developed a simple calendar based upon the phases of the moon, but the solar calendar was far superior and surprisingly accurate.

The calendar was worked out during the Old Kingdom by an elite group of intellectuals paid by the government. These early scientists divided the year into three seasons: the flooding of the Nile (the Inundation), the planting season (the Reemergence) and the dry season (the Drought). The new year began around July 20th at the onset of the Inundation. They further subdivided the year into twelve months of thirty days (based upon the cycles of the moon). But this created a problem, since their twelve months ended five days short of a solar year. The disparity became apparent to everyone after a few years, when the Inundation seemed to occur increasingly ahead of schedule. Once the matter was sorted out, the priests (the truly learned men of ancient Egypt) created a myth to justify adding five extra days to the end of the year. According to the myth, Thoth, the god of wisdom and writing, played a game of dice with the moon. When Thoth won, the moon had to give the world five extra days and moonlit evenings in recompense. The Egyptians used these extra days for religious festivals and general merry-making.

The calendar was still slightly off, however, since it did not account for the extra quarter of a day required to complete one revolution of the earth around the sun. However, it was the most accurate measurement of time the ancient world had ever known. Every few years the priests added an extra day or two (occasions for more religious celebrations) to realign the first appearance of Sirius with the start of the Inundation. The Egyptian calendar was later adopted by Julius Caesar in the first century B.C.E. for use throughout the Roman Empire, and it is the model for the one we use today.

Once they knew when to expect the Inundation, the Egyptians could deal with the problem of predicting the level of the flood. They knew that higher floodwaters than usual meant damage to the dikes and destruction of the villages that were built on the edge of the floodplain. A low level produced a poor harvest, since not enough land was saturated with water and fertilized with silt. Also, too little water was left behind in the catch basins to irrigate the innermost fields. To predict the volume of the flood, the

Part of an ancient calendar found on a tomb wall

Along the banks of the Nile

Egyptians invented the Nilometer, a stone gauge with lines cut into it to measure the rate at which the river was rising. Nilometers were placed upriver near the First Cataract. When the river began to rise, the level was carefully measured and recorded. The information was passed on to farmers living down river by messengers traveling in swift papyrus boats. Although the farmers could not control the level of flooding, at least they could make appropriate preparations for the effects it would have on their land.

Measuring the Land

The Egyptians applied their knowledge of the stars to the design of their construction projects. For example, the plan for a pyramid required that the four sides of its base face north, south, east and west. The architects reasoned that once they found true north, they could easily determine the other three directions. But how to find north? They resolved this problem by building a tall circle of stones at the site of the pyramid. A priest spent about twelve dark hours in the center of the circle, noting where a particular star rose in the evening and set in the morning. (He must have napped in between.) He

carefully marked these points on the rocks— exactly halfway between them was true north.

The Egyptians needed to survey and measure the land along the Nile in order to determine the taxes owed by the farmers. And every year as the Nile receded they had to redefine the boundaries of the farmers' fields. Of course, there were boundary stones, and it was a serious crime to move one of them, but the flood waters often shifted them out of position. Surveyors determined the dimensions of the fields by using ropes laid out in straight lines. Knots were tied on the ropes at certain intervals just as lines are drawn to mark off inches and feet on a yardstick. A field would be so many knots wide and so many knots long. The surveyors were known as the "rope stretchers."

The Egyptians also understood basic principles of geometry, such as how to measure right angles or how to determine the area of rectangles, squares, and triangles. They could even calculate the area of a circle, which they divided into 360 degrees, just as we do today. In fact, the small circle used as a sign for degrees is actually an Egyptian hieroglyph. Measurements had to be precise, since the farmers had to pay their taxes (in produce) according to the area of their property. Of course, a knowledge of geometry was essential for the design and construction of the pyramids.

Early Mathematics

The Egyptians' understanding of the concepts of the measurement of time and space assumed a basic knowledge of mathematics. The earliest Nile dwellers probably chipped notches on pieces of wood or stone to record the passing of time or the number of their possessions. Later on, hieroglyphic symbols were used to represent numbers. The Egyptian method of counting was based on the number ten, probably because human beings have ten fingers and ten toes with which to count. The numbers one through nine were represented by small lines (two lines for number two, etc.); ten was a human heel (an upward semicircle), one hundred was a coiled rope, one thousand was a flower, ten thousand was a pointing finger, one hundred thousand was a tadpole, and one million was a man with his hands lifted toward the sky. There were also symbols for fractions. An oval meant "one part of," and so an oval written above a heel meant one part of ten or one tenth.

Objects were measured in cubits. A cubit was the length of the human forearm from the elbow to the tip of the middle finger. Originally, a cubit was based on the forearm of the reigning pharaoh, but since pharaohs came in different sizes, a more standardized measuring stick was eventually created. Other measurements were based upon the width of a human palm and a finger. Four fingers equaled one palm, and seven palms equaled one cubit.

Objects were weighed on balance scales. A stone or stones were placed on one side of the scale and the object was placed on the other. The object weighed so many stones. By the Middle Kingdom, a fixed weight in gold, silver or copper was used in business transactions. This weight was called a deben. A sack of barley, for example, would weigh a certain number of deben. This was the closest the Egyptians ever came to having a currency.

Egyptian numerals.

The Study of Human Anatomy

Perhaps the greatest contribution made to science by the Egyptians lay in the field of biology (the study of living things). The priests who prepared corpses for burial learned a great deal about human anatomy as they removed the vital organs. Yet, their religious beliefs prevented them from dissecting a body any more than was necessary for mummification—to do otherwise was considered sinful. This superstition severely limited their ability to understand the functioning of the human body, and they continued to believe that the heart, and not the brain, was the center of thought and emotion.

Nonetheless, the Egyptians were for a long time the best physicians of the ancient world. Their knowledge came not only from studying the dead but also from close observation of the living. They noted the symptoms of various illnesses, and through trial and error they determined the effectiveness of specific drugs. They experimented with herbs, spices and minerals, as well as animal products like honey and goose grease. They recognized the value of castor oil in treating an upset stomach. They prescribed the pods of the poppy plant to pacify a cranky baby. (This was an effective pacifier, since poppies are the source of opium!) Certain remedies, however, such as turtle brains and crushed donkey hooves, were of little value. Nor was the so-called painkiller made from animal fat and cattle dung slowly swallowed with beer.

Egyptian physicians followed a scientific method. They observed the patient, examined the source of physical discomfort, diagnosed the problem, and then prescribed treatment, just as doctors do today. They recorded their observations on papyrus scrolls; these were the first medical textbooks in history.

Poppies

The Egyptians knew how to set broken bones and attach a splint. They sawed through skulls with copper tools to treat headaches (by relieving pressure on the brain), and they amputated badly infected limbs. They even successfully removed tumors. Egyptian doctors were the first to use bandages and compresses. They knew about infections, although not about antibiotics. And they understood the importance of bed rest and hygiene to prevent the complications of illness.

Egyptian dentists knew how to pull teeth and treat gum infections. They filled cavities with malachite, frankincense and yellow ochre, and they even made false teeth from those that they pulled.

Unfortunately, religion continued to play an important part in the treatment of patients and it impeded the development of medical science. Physicians often chanted and recited spells, and they drew "magic circles" around their patients' houses to chase off evil spirits. Frequently the patient himself was told to chant certain words at fixed intervals of time while rattling magic charms. Surprisingly, the treatment often worked, because a large part of getting better depends upon a person's belief that he is improving.

Questions

1. How did the Egyptians use the stars to predict the Inundation?

2. How accurate was the Egyptian solar calendar?

3. How did the Egyptians measure the hours of the day?

4. What was a "rope stretcher?"

5. How would the Egyptians write 1,125?

6. What is a cubit?

7. What advances did Egyptian physicians make in the field of prescribed medications?

8. What did the Egyptians know of dentistry?

9. What effect did Egyptian religion have on the development of medical knowledge?

10. Who wrote the first medical books in history?

Further Thoughts

1. Although the Egyptians designed a very accurate calendar to mark the seasons, their system of recording the years was based upon political events. They numbered the years from the beginning of a pharaoh's reign, and when he died they started counting all over again. It took a long time for historians to shuffle through the ancient records and accurately date the events that took place during three thousand years of Egyptian history!

2. Scribes measuring the amount of grain owed to the temple granary often used the eye of Horus as a symbol for fractions. Each part of the famous eye represented a certain fraction. For example: The eyebrow represented one eighth, the white to the left of the iris was one half, that to the right was one sixteenth, the iris itself was one fourth, the tear below the eye was one sixty-fourth, and the curling lash was one thirty-second. If you add all the fractions together, you get only 63/64. That is because 1/64 of the

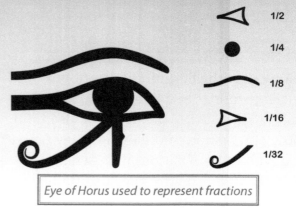

1/2
1/4
1/8
1/16
1/32

Eye of Horus used to represent fractions

eye represents the magic that helped restore vision to Horus!

Projects

1. Be a "rope-stretcher." Using a string or rope with knots at appropriate intervals, measure the number of cubits in the length and width of your classroom, or the dimensions of the hall corridor. Measure other articles in the classroom in cubits, palms, and digits.

2. Make a water clock using a large plastic or Styrofoam bowl. Make some holes and experiment to determine the rate at which the water flows out. Then mark the hours on the inside of the bowl with indelible ink.

3. The builders of the pyramids knew that they could make a perfect square corner by using a knotted rope. Try it yourself. Take a piece of string or rope and divide it into twelve equal parts. Knot it after the first three parts, and then after the next four parts and again after the next five. With friends standing at the third, seventh and twelfth knots, arrange the rope in a triangle on the floor (the longest part is the hypotenuse). These measurements will produce a perfect right triangle every time!

CHAPTER 9

EVERYDAY LIFE

The Nile valley appears today much as it did five thousand years ago. The sky is always clear and blue, the river vegetation is lush, and the dryness of the air makes the desert heat tolerable. Villages and towns still nestle along the boundary where fertile field meets desert sand, and farmers still use many of the devices that were invented nearly five thousand years ago, such as the shaduf and the wooden plow. It is not unusual to see an ox plodding around a circular path by the river's edge. As it moves, it pulls on a wooden spoke, which in turn activates a primitive water wheel. You've probably seen pictures of water wheels that were used by colonial flour mills—the design hasn't changed much after all these centuries. The Egyptian farmers attach buckets to the wheel, and as it turns around, the buckets scoop up water from the river and carry it up to the level of the fields. The water is poured into shallow irrigation ditches or onto the crops. Then the buckets are carried down to the water again by the wheel, and the process is repeated.

The mud-brick houses that border the fields today closely resemble those of ancient times. Even the bricks themselves are made in the same way as they were in ancient times. Mud is scooped from the Nile, mixed with chopped straw or sand, and then poured into rectangular wooden molds. These are left to dry in the hot sun until the mud hardens. Finally the bricks are tapped out of the molds and carted off to a building site.

Although there are a few large cities in modern Egypt (Cairo, the capital, is the largest city in Africa), most of the people live in the rural areas and work in the fields as their ancestors did long ago. So much about the landscape and daily routine has remained unchanged over the millennia that a visit to the Nile Valley or a glance at a picture book of the modern country reveal a great deal about the everyday lives of the ancient Egyptians.

Remains Provide Clues to the Past

Archaeologists have learned much from studying the ruins of the abandoned city of Akhenaten (its modern name is Dar el Amarna) and those of a village once inhabited by workmen who built the tombs in the Valley of the Kings (Deir el Medina). Akhenaten's city, buried by desert sands soon after his death, holds many clues about the lives of the royalty and nobility of the New Kingdom, while the workmen's village provides evidence about the living conditions of the ordinary people. Sites of other towns and settlements are continually being uncovered and studied. Archaeologists have found many tools and artifacts, and

Farming village and fields along the Nile

even some remnants of plywood—as far as we know, Egyptian carpenters were the first to work with this manmade building material.

Of course, the wall paintings and the articles placed in the tombs for use in the Afterlife are an invaluable source of information about daily life in ancient Egypt. Despite the tomb robberies, the paintings and many of the objects have survived, including statuettes (models) of Egyptians performing everyday tasks, such as grinding wheat and making bread. And discoveries continue to be made beneath the sands of Egypt. In October of 2010, an elaborate tomb was found in a cliff near the Great Pyramids of Giza. It belonged to a priest who was in charge of performing purification rituals for the dead pharaoh Khafre. It was filled with artwork and artifacts that enrich our understanding of the ancient culture.

Housing in Early Times

The houses of the farmers and craftsmen of earliest times were small and compact. During the Old Kingdom, the mud-brick walls were strengthened at intervals by columns made from bunches of papyrus reeds. These reeds were first tied together and filled with mud. Once the mud dried in the hot sun, the column became hard and fairly sturdy. These were the forerunners of the stone columns used in the great temples of later years. The stone pillars were often fluted, imitating the design of the bunches of reeds that had supported the roofs of the humble villagers.

The buildings in the towns were narrow and crowded together because land was scarce. The windows in a typical house were

Engraving of an Egyptian house

small and placed near the ceiling to allow ventilation while cutting down on the heat of the sun. In the evening, light was provided by a lamp consisting of a pottery bowl filled with olive oil and a wick. Facing toward the street was an outer room, often used as a workshop. The living area was in the center of the house. Beyond that was a bedroom and the kitchen. The inner walls of the house were plain, usually plastered and painted white.

A staircase led to the roof where the family often spent the night because it was cooler than inside. There was little danger of rain, and often there was a refreshing breeze. Cooking was also done outside in domed clay ovens to lessen the risk of fire as well as to keep the extra heat away from the interior of the house. In the daytime, an awning was opened on the roof to provide shade. Below, a small courtyard served as a granary and a place to keep the family's animals at night.

The few pieces of furniture would include a stool or two, a table, and wooden chests for storage. There are not many trees in Egypt, and so wood had to be imported. For this reason, each piece of furniture was greatly valued. Most furnishings were made from the wood of acacias, sycamores, palms, and willows. Red cedar from Byblos and black ebony from Nubia were luxury materials that only the rich could afford.

An Egyptian bed consisted of a wooden frame to which was attached a woven rush mat and a footboard. The bed sloped slightly downward from head to foot. Bedcovers were made of woven linen. Awkward looking wooden headrests actually served a useful purpose. At bedtime, an Egyptian placed a soft pillow on his headrest and lay down. During the night the air freely circulated around his neck while his face was somewhat protected from any scorpion that might wander in!

The Estates of the Nobility

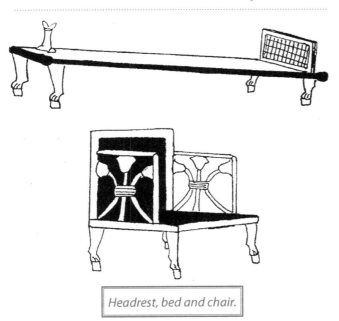

Headrest, bed and chair.

In sharp contrast to the humble dwellings of the ordinary people were the large and spacious homes of the wealthy. The buildings and grounds of these estates often covered more than an acre of land. They were surrounded by thick walls to insure privacy and prevent curious passersby from peeking in! Just within the walls of an estate there would be a pleasant courtyard shaded by date palms and imported trees such as acacias, willows, tamarisks and pomegranates. These trees were watered frequently to keep their foliage full and lush. Stone-lined ornamental ponds were stocked with an array of colorful goldfish. Family dogs (sleek grey-hounds), cats and even imported monkeys frolicked about the courtyard in complete freedom to amuse and entertain the inhabitants and their guests. There might be a terrace built of limestone overlooking the Nile.

The floors of the house were raised to discourage the entry of the cobras that lived in the river marshes. Inside, the mud-brick walls were covered with white plaster and beautifully painted with colorful frescoes of birds, plants, fish and animals. Graceful wooden pillars helped to support the roof. Artfully displayed about the house would be stone or pottery vases of papyrus flowers or bowls of water upon which floated lotus blossoms. The flower display depended upon the location of the house. Papyrus grew most abundantly in the delta of Lower Egypt, while the lotus flourished in the narrow valley to the south. The rooms were furnished with handsome wooden tables, leather chairs, couches with soft cushions of feathers covered with fine linen, and chests inlaid with ebony or cedar and often decorated with gold leaf. There were even indoor toilets containing chamber pots, which were emptied into the nearest canal. Beginning in the Middle Kingdom, slaves (usually the children of foreigners captured in wars) did the housework and waited upon the master and his family.

Behind the house were the servants' quarters, stables for the horses that drew the hunting chariots, and stalls for cattle that were being fattened for the table. Pigeons were kept in an aviary. There were also workshops for weavers, carpenters, bakers, brewers, butchers, and other specialists who labored for the master of the estate. Beyond the gates stretched fields of wheat and barley. Even the smaller estates were remarkably self-sufficient, and those of the viziers and nomarchs resembled mini-kingdoms.

What the Egyptians Looked Like

The typical Egyptian was slight of stature, rather short (men were less than five feet six inches tall while women were about five feet), dark complexioned (like a modern Arab), black-haired, with a long, somewhat bird-like face. Based on their studies of mummies, archaeologists estimate that the average life span along the Nile in those early times was between thirty-five and forty years.

This painting of a hunting scene shows the typical dress of man, woman, and child.

Wooden sculpture of an Egyptian man

Most Egyptian clothing was made from linen, a material woven from the fibers of the flax plant. The texture of the cloth varied from a course weave to a fine, nearly transparent fabric. The finer the weave, the more desirable (and expensive) the cloth. The men of the upper classes wore kilts (short skirts that tied at the waist), and the women wore long, straight dresses that were held up by two straps and fell gracefully to the ankles. On cool evenings, the women wore colorful woolen shawls. Nearly everyone wore sandals made of papyrus reeds, although a nobleman might own a pair made of soft leather. This basic attire changed very little for three thousand years (in the New Kingdom the kilts and dresses were slightly more elaborate). A peasant man wore only a coarse linen loincloth called a *daiu* to work in the hot sun, and children up to the age of eight usually wore nothing at all.

Man and woman wearing wigs

Jewelry and Wigs

Men as well as women loved jewelry—earrings (they pierced their ears), necklaces, rings, bracelets and anklets—and they wore it whenever they could. Wealthy Egyptians wore jewelry made of gold, silver and semiprecious stones such as turquoise and lapis lazuli. Ordinary people wore necklaces and bracelets of glazed beads made of crushed limestone (called faience), shells and polished pebbles. The poorest people wore chains made of flowers. In addition to its decorative value, the jewelry was believed to have protective powers against everyday dangers and even death.

Perhaps because of the effects of the intense heat of the desert, the Egyptians disdained long hair. Men had their heads shaved from time to time, letting their hair grow to about one inch before shaving it again. Over their short hair the wealthy Egyptians wore elaborate wigs made from human hair or sheep wool and kept in place with beeswax. Not only were the wigs considered the height of fashion, but they also offered protection against the intense

rays of the sun. Children of the upper classes had all but one sidelock of hair shaved off.

Cosmetics

The Egyptians were very fastidious people. We have learned that the priests shaved every part of their bodies. Ordinary people bathed frequently, and they shaved their arms and legs with hooked bronze razors. Since they had no soap, they used oil for shaving. They plucked their eyebrows with tweezers. Both men and women used cosmetics. They applied scented oils to their bodies to prevent the skin from drying in the desert heat and they outlined their eyes with Kohl (a black sticky mixture made from galena, a sulfide of lead). This made the eyes appear very large, and it protected them from the glare of the sun. (Today baseball and football players smear dark grease on their cheekbones below their eyes to cut down the sun's glare on the playing field.) Green coloring made from malachite (an oxide of copper) was applied to the eyelids for similar purposes. Women mixed red ochre powder (made from oxides of iron) with animal fat to form a paste used to rouge their cheeks and paint their lips. Red henna was the basic ingredient of a polish applied to toe and finger nails. Sometimes it was rubbed into the palms of the hands and the soles of the feet. All this makeup required the use of small hand mirrors of polished bronze or copper. Perfume, liberally applied over the entire body, was made from myrrh and frankincense (the resins of trees imported from Punt) and squeezed lotus blossoms.

A wealthy Egyptian woman

Entertainment Among the Nobility

The wealthy Egyptians loved to have parties. When the guests arrived for a festive occasion at a nobleman's villa, servants placed cones of perfumed animal fat upon their heads. This would melt during the evening, sending trickles of sweet-smelling lotion over their wigs and shoulders. This was considered a pleasant sensation in the desert heat, although it must have made a bit of a sticky mess as it dripped onto their linen attire! The guests sat upon chairs or mats of woven papyrus reeds. Servants also placed garlands of flowers around their shoulders and replaced the cones as they melted.

The Nile valley offered a bountiful variety of dishes for the meal. The wealthy enjoyed such delicacies as roast duck and goose and broiled ox, accompanied by lentils and chickpeas cooked in herbs and spices, lettuce and radishes, figs and watermelon, sweet cakes saturated with honey, and date or grape wine. Pig was considered unfit to eat, probably because its flesh goes bad quickly if it is not refrigerated. The food was cooked in clay ovens or over open fires. It was often fried in sesame oil. Favorite seasonings were garlic, cumin, coriander, and parsley. The fact that many mummies have badly decayed teeth suggests that they may have overindulged in sweets!

The people ate with their fingers, helping themselves to food served on large pottery platters. Servants constantly poured water

Women with cones of perfumed fat

from jugs over the greasy hands of the diners, who held their hands above a small basin. They dried their hands with soft linen towels.

After a meal, the men often sipped a liqueur called grenadine made from pomegranates. Grenadine is a popular liqueur even today. Entertainment was provided by dancers, acrobats, or musicians playing harps, flutes and lutes. The festivities could last into the early hours of the morning.

The Meals of the Common People

The meals of the ordinary people were far humbler. The staple of their diet was bread made from wheat or barley flour. In fact, the average man ate ten (small) loaves of bread a day! There were many varieties and shapes of the loaves, and often they were sweetened with honey and dates. The Egyptians were the first to enjoy the taste of raisin bread. Unfortunately, they unknowingly consumed a large amount of grit (ground up stone) that got mixed with the flour when the wheat was ground by a soft millstone. Probably a few grains of sand were occasionally blown into the dough as well. We know about this because the teeth of many mummies appear to have been worn down from a diet of gritty food! Everyone ate salads, to which onions and papyrus sprouts were often added for variety. On special occasions, the ordinary people ate fish from the Nile and game birds that had been caught in nets, followed by a serving of fresh fruit.

Egyptian Beverages

The wine that the upper classes enjoyed came from grapes grown upon trellises on estates in the delta. Clay jars have been found that bear labels similar to those placed on modern wine bottles. A typical ancient label listed the name of the estate where the grapes were grown, its location, the specific vineyard, the vintner (the man who produced the wine), the date, and an assessment of the wine's quality. Wines were rated as follows: good, twice good, three times good, genuine, and sweet. Poor quality wine was designated "for merry-making." Apparently 1344 B.C.E. was a very good year for red wine.

Adults of the middle and lower classes usually drank beer. This was made from barley bread crumbs that were mixed with water and honey and left to ferment for several days. It was not unusual to consume two jugs of beer a day. Fortunately, the alcoholic content was far less than that of modern beer! The rich drank beer with ordinary meals but preferred wine with special dinners. Children drank goats' milk. (Most of the milk was made into cheese so that it wouldn't spoil in the heat.)

Leisure Pastimes

The Egyptians amused themselves in many ways. Wealthy young men enjoyed hunting in the desert. Armed with bows and arrows (in the New Kingdom they drove horse-drawn chariots), they chased antelopes and gazelles as well as lions and leopards. Dogs were trained to flush out the prey. Often lion cubs were caught and trained to run alongside the chariot of the pharaoh. Ramses the Great had just such a "pet."

There was also an unlimited supply of game in the Nile itself—fish, ducks and geese, alligators, and hippopotami. The

The pharaoh hunts birds along the Nile

hippopotami were pests that trampled the farmers' fields, but they were the targets of only the bravest hunters. Remember, King Menes died from the infection caused when he was wounded by a hippopotamus!

The hunters maneuvered small papyrus rafts among the reeds until they could spear or net small river dwellers. Sometimes they fished using hooks made from bone or ivory. Birds were stunned by throwing sticks resembling boomerangs. Cats often went along on the river hunts and, according to the stories painted on the walls of the tombs, they retrieved the fallen prey for their masters. Like the tigers of Java, the Egyptian cats apparently loved water.

The river was also the site of competitive games. One game involved a group of young men standing up in small, highly unstable papyrus boats. Each was armed with a long wooden pole, and his goal was to push his opponent into the water. They had a great incentive to stay afloat, since the Nile was teeming with crocodiles and snakes. Other less dangerous competitions took place on land. The Egyptians loved to watch chariot races and wrestling matches, and they placed bets upon their favorites.

Quieter forms of entertainment included board games. One of the treasures discovered in King Tut's tomb was a game called Senet. Similar to Parchesi, it was placed there for the young king to wile away the hours of eternity. Several other board games have also been found in tombs, including one similar to our modern game of Chutes and Ladders.

Playthings changed very little over the millennia until the advent of modern

A hippo shows off its tusks

technology, and Egyptian children had their share of dolls, tops, leather balls, and wooden animals with moving parts.

A favorite game of active boys was called "goat on the ground." To play it, two boys would sit on the ground facing each other with their legs stretched out. Opponents had to jump over their legs without being caught. Different versions of this game are still played by children throughout the modern world.

The Egyptians enjoyed music, and we have learned about their instruments. The earliest account in history of a full orchestra took place in Egypt during a religious festival in 250 B.C.E. Six hundred musicians performed for the pharaoh, Ptolemy.

When the sun set in ancient Egypt, a family would often gather, perhaps inside by an oil lamp, or more likely, on the roof of their house in the light of the stars and the moon. This was a perfect time for storytelling. The choices were many, since the Egyptians had a rich literature of myths about the gods and goddesses, heroic legends of the exploits of the pharaohs, and old-fashioned adventure stories. A popular story of the Middle Kingdom was about Sinuhe, an Egyptian outcast who had many adventures in faraway Syria and Palestine before he finally returned to the Nile Valley. Another favorite tale described the wanderings of a ship-wrecked sailor, whom many scholars identify as the original Sinbad the Sailor.

Families Ties

Family life was important to the ancient Egyptians. Many tomb paintings show couples sharing peaceful moments, and stone statues often portray the woman tenderly holding her arm around her husband. Although the pharaoh had many wives, most Egyptians were monogamous (had one spouse). A man could choose his wife, but she had the right to refuse him. Once married, a woman was responsible for running the household. In fact, the property was put in her name, and on the death of her husband she inherited the house and the land. Those marriages that did not work out ended in divorce. A divorced man was obligated to support his wife until she remarried. Children were treated affectionately.

Life along the Nile seems to have been satisfying for every class of Egyptians—the sun always shone brightly, harvests were bountiful, and the pharaoh usually provided peace and harmony. It is not surprising that the Egyptians wanted such a pleasant life style to last for eternity.

Questions

1. In what ways does modern Egypt resemble ancient times?
2. What discoveries made in Deir el Medina help us to understand life in ancient Egypt?
3. Why did the Egyptians spend much of their time on the roofs of their houses?
4. Why was wooden furniture greatly valued?
5. Describe the estate of an Egyptian nobleman.
6. What was Egyptian jewelry like?
7. What was the purpose of a cone of animal fat?
8. Describe the meal of a peasant family.

9. What do you know about Egyptian literature?

10. What was the role of an Egyptian woman?

Further Thoughts

1. Not much is left of the towns of the delta region. In addition to the destruction of organic materials caused by rapid decay in that moist environment, local peasants used to hunt for "sebakh" (the decomposed mud-bricks of ancient buildings), which they dug up and used for fertilizer!

Nor did Upper Egypt escape the devastation of archaeological treasures by the native population. During the early Christian era, Coptic monks commonly used chisels and sledge-hammers to hack off the heads and limbs of ancient statues and to deface the inscriptions of the "pagan" pharaohs.

2. The Egyptians were often intrigued by people who were born with unusual physical characteristics—in particular dwarfs (they called them *nmiu*) and pygmies (*dng*). Such individuals performed in religious festivals and were often servants to the pharaoh. Archaeologists have found the remains of fifty dwarfs. In 1990 the remains of a dwarf who had been the cupbearer to Khafre were found in a tomb near the second great pyramid. He was named Pyrnyankhu, and he was hunch-backed with a large head and very short legs.

Projects

1. Plan and enjoy an Egyptian feast with your classmates. This is an opportunity to wear ample amounts of make-up and jewelry. Simple articles of clothing can be fashioned from old white sheets. Study the descriptions of the food and table manners in this chapter, and come up with your own version. After the meal, someone should read the story of Sinbad the Sailor or the myth of Osiris and Seth.

2. Learn more about Egyptian columns. Then find out about the basic structure of the pillars of ancient Greece and compare them with those of Egypt. Write a short report and draw illustrations of the Egyptian and Greek columns.

3. Make a diorama of the estate of a wealthy Egyptian.

4. Find out more about Egyptian jewelry. Write a short, illustrated report. Make your own models of bracelets and necklaces using string and clay.

EPILOGUE

The civilization of Egypt had been the richest and longest lived in the history of the ancient world. But nothing lasts forever. As we learned in Chapter 3, the central government fell apart at the end of the New Kingdom, and Egypt was taken over by invading armies - Persians, Greeks, Romans, and finally Arabs. The rule of each succeeding foreign leader effectively whittled away at what was left of local Egyptian culture until almost nothing of it remained in the Nile Valley. Fortunately, many of the ideas and inventions of Egypt were adopted by other civilizations of the Mediterranean world and the ancient texts were translated into their languages. They remain an important influence on our own modern western culture.

"The Gift of the Nile"

Ancient Egypt could never have existed without the gently flowing river that snakes its way through the barren stretches of desert. Herodotus's description of Egypt as "the gift of the Nile" couldn't have been more accurate. Not only did the river nourish the lush vegetation that grew along its banks and enrich the soil as it annually rose twenty-five feet above its normal level, it also forced the local inhabitants to make decisions and experiment with innovations that resulted in a highly sophisticated civilization. The river became a central artery linking the string of settlements that sprung up along its banks. The geography of the valley made it easy for a strong leader to gain and manage control over large numbers of

people. The river pervaded every aspect of the culture of ancient Egypt. It determined the course of development of its economy, its religion, its government, and even its art.

As we conclude the story of Ancient Egypt, let's review some of the highlights of that rich civilization's contributions to world culture. Advances in writing, for example. The need to keep track of the taxes paid by the farmers led to the development of a written language. In later years, the Egyptians paid back their debt to the merchants of the Middle East (who taught them about cuneiform) when their hieroglyphs inspired another nation, the Phoenicians, to create the world's first alphabet. This, in turn, was the model for the Greek alphabet, which ultimately served as the basis of our own.

The efforts by Egyptian astronomers to predict the Inundation produced the solar calendar that is the model for the one used throughout the modern world. And the need to redefine the boundaries of the farmers' fields induced Egyptian surveyors to perform calculations that led to a greater understanding of basic principles of mathematics and geometry. The pyramids could never have been built without a mastery of these principles as well as a strong government that could organize thousands of workers. And the art of embalming bodies was the first step in understanding human anatomy and physiology.

Egypt's religious traditions were closely bound to the patterns of the river. The cycle of the planting of seeds, harvesting of crops, withering of the old plants, and then replanting of seeds was reflected in the farmers' hopes for an afterlife. For just as a child grew to be a man or woman, had a family, worked hard into old age, and died, his body could be preserved so that his soul could enjoy a new life in a better place. Remarkably, it was Akhenaten's turning from the traditional religion by worshipping a single god that ties us most directly to ancient Egypt. Not long after the death of the "heretic Pharaoh" (Akhenaten), a Middle Eastern people, the Hebrews, began to worship a single deity. Many scholars believe that there was a cross-fertilization of the religious beliefs of the Egyptians and the Hebrews. Christianity later evolved from the Hebrew religion (Judaism). Islam, founded by Muhammad in the seventh century C.E., is also based upon the worship of a single deity and shares many core beliefs and principles with Judaism and Christianity.

The stone monuments of ancient Egypt—the tombs, temples, colossal statues and obelisks—are stately and majestic. Their orderly design influenced the architects of later Mediterranean cultures. The bundles of mud-caked papyrus reeds that supported the walls of the ancient houses in the Nile valley were the first stage in a long process of experimentation and innovation that ultimately resulted in the graceful columns of classical buildings.

The Egyptians hoped that life as they knew it in the warm and pleasant valley of the Nile would last for eternity. In a sense, this wish has been granted, because so many of their ideas as well as their art, artifacts, and stone monuments have survived the centuries and remain a permanent testimony of their rich civilization.

Further Thoughts

1. Herodotus has been mentioned frequently throughout this book, and perhaps a few words ought to be said here about his works. As we have learned, he was a Greek who visited ancient Egypt in the fifth century B.C.E. Because he was the first person to write about the geography, customs and historical events of a foreign culture, he is considered the Father of History. Herodotus visited Egypt after the decline of the New Kingdom, a time when the pyramids had stood for over two thousand years. The Old Kingdom probably seemed nearly as far removed in time from him as it does from us today.

Herodotus' written work (*The History*) contains a large section devoted to Egypt that provides modern scholars with valuable eyewitness observations. However, he had an unfortunate tendency to allow his own biases to influence his interpretation of historical events, and he frequently came to conclusions that have since been proven inaccurate. Nonetheless, Herodotus introduced Greek scholars to the richness of Egyptian culture and sparked in them an appreciation for the extraordinary accomplishments of the Nile dwellers.

2. Alexandria, a city founded in the delta by Alexander the Great in the fourth century B.C.E., became a great center of learning in the Mediterranean world. Greek was the official language of the city, and many of the Egyptian scholarly works were translated into Greek. In fact, Greek became the official language of all of Egypt. Of all the rulers of Ptolemy's dynasty, only one (the famous Cleopatra) ever bothered to learn the language of the Egyptians. This

explains why so many people, places and things of importance in Egyptian history bear Greek names. For example, the pharaohs that were buried in the three pyramids of Giza are known to many by their Greek names: Cheops (Khufu), Chefren (Khafre) and Mycerinus (Menkaure). Even the word "Egypt" comes from the Greek name for the Nile Delta and Valley—*Aigyptos*.

Although the Egyptians must have been exasperated by the way the Greeks took over their nation, historians today are thankful that they did so. Many of the ideas of the ancient Nile dwellers might have been lost if the Greeks had not carefully translated them into their own language on rolls of papyrus later stored in Alexandria. And, of course, let's not forget that the key to deciphering Egyptian hieroglyphs was the Greek writing on the Rosetta Stone.

3. Many of the plants and creatures that thrived in ancient Egypt are no longer found there. For example, hippopotami and crocodiles cannot be found further north than Sudan. Attempts have been made recently to reintroduce papyrus plants into the delta area. Perhaps conservationists will eventually be able to restore many parts of the natural environment of ancient Egypt.

The construction of the Aswan dam ended the annual inundations of the Nile. As a result, the soil of the floodplain is no longer naturally revitalized with silt, and it has to be fertilized artificially. This, unfortunately, has led to great accumulations of salt in the soil, and the "black land" is not as productive as it was in ancient times.

Projects

1. Egyptology (the study of ancient Egypt) began when Napoleon's men invaded Egypt in the nineteenth century. Research the activities of the French army in Egypt and write a short report discussing their contribution to our understanding of the civilization of that ancient land.

2. On poster board, make an illustrated list of the contributions of the ancient Egyptians to our modern culture.

3. Modern Egypt is a vital nation in the Middle East. Consult an almanac or encyclopedia to find out who the current leaders are.

4. Visit the Egyptian collection in the city museum nearest you.

5. The most exciting archaeological find in Egypt since King Tut's tomb was the labyrinth of chambers serving as the tomb of Ramses II's fifty-two sons. It was discovered in the Valley of the Kings in 1995. Consult your library and the Internet to find out more about this fascinating discovery.

TIMELINE

(dates are approximate)

5000 B.C.E.	Nomads settle along the banks of the Nile
4000 B.C.E.	Establishment of nomes and the rule of nomarchs
3500 B.C.E.	Agriculture fully established in the Nile valley
3300 B.C.E.	Solidification of the kingdoms of Upper and Lower Egypt
3100 B.C.E.	Menes unifies Upper and Lower Egypt
3100 - 2700 B.C.E.	The Archaic Period
2700 - 2200 B.C.E.	The Old Kingdom: The Age of the Pyramids
2100 B.C.E.	First Intermediate Period: Civil war and chaos
2000 - 1700 B.C.E.	The Middle Kingdom: The expansion of trade
1700 B.C.E.	Second Intermediate Period: The Hyksos invasion
1500 - 1000 B.C.E.	The New Kingdom: The Empire
1000 B.C.E.	Decline: Egypt is divided, then ruled by priests and foreign princes
525 B.C.E.	Invasion by the Persians
330 B.C.E. - 342 C.E.	Greek and Roman Periods
640 C.E.	Arab Conquest

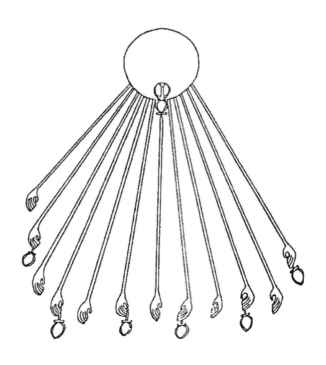

INDEX